Pr

"As a medical missionary who lived and worked in the Amoy area of Fukien Province in Southeast China during the last days of the Nationalist regime in China and the early days of the People's (Communist) Republic of China (1947-1951), I read this book with much interest. It presented an opportunity to compare my experience with the author's experience garnered about one hundred miles north of Amoy in Foochow in the same province. She and her husband arrived there to teach in the mission's Foochow College from 1926 to 1932. At this time, there was another transition in which the young Nationalist Party was moving north against warlords and an equally young Communist Party then being led and encouraged by Russian Communist prompters. Her excellent portrayals of what she saw and experienced were much more life-threatening than what my wife and I experienced. She uses dialogue deftly to describe the anxious and tense periods during which the angry crowds of anti-Americans presented danger at the school and in the market place. The opportunity to know what life was like for American teachers in that period and in that country has been made available in this short but exciting book, written by Elizabeth Shrader with her son's help."

—Jack W. Hill, M.D.
Penney Farms,
FL
May 20, 2012

"a wonderful read.... a unique account of how missionaries and students thought about religions and communism..."

—George D. Ngu,
Foochow Mission Historian

"At that time in history (1927—-), Nationalism and Revolution, the conversations of this young couple share noble thoughts & lofty goals that readers can identify with.

"...the sleeping dragon that was waking up and would shake the world. China—what a mess the white man had made out there. And we are supposed to 'have God' and be a 'Christian country'!" (Calls to remember the shame of the Opium wars, blaming England, but also America.)

"Don't want to be a 'missionary.' That's too pious. It makes me sound better than I really am. We're not going to China to snatch souls from a hot hell. Not the old motive-salvation. Not just 'personal salvation', but what we can DO to end hatred between nations in the world."

"Desire to work with students, helping them become world-minded leaders that believe that nationalism must be the stepping stone to Internationalism, so that all countries work together for the good of the whole world."

"As educators, you are redefining "salvation" as wholeness and highest possible fulfillments."

"As a woman, I want to discover; make friends with people who have been calling white men 'foreign devils' for a century. With reason, of course."

—Alma Bjork-Olson

"*Magic Peach* is a delightful first-hand journey of early 20th century life in old Foochow, Friar Odoric's (1323-1327) 'great city upon the sea.' A city of contrasts, the 2200-year-old cradle of maritime ship building drew Chinese and foreign merchants, adventurers, diplomats and missionaries, but was also home to the free-spirited scholars who built China's first public library, and whom Marco Polo claimed the Great Khan kept in line only by stationing a large garrison in the heart of the banyan-covered city. The world forgot Old Foochow after Liberation in 1949, but *Magic Peach* reawakens the magic.

—Professor Bill Brown, Xiamen University

Taste This Magic Peach

Taste This Magic Peach

An Educator's Life in China During the Nationalist Revolution

Elizabeth Hand Shrader

with William Whitney Shrader

TATE PUBLISHING
AND ENTERPRISES, LLC

Taste This Magic Peach

Published by Tate Publishing & Enterprises, LLC
127 E. Trade Center Terrace | Mustang, Oklahoma 73064 USA
1.888.361.9473 | www.tatepublishing.com

Tate Publishing is committed to excellence in the publishing industry. The company reflects the philosophy established by the founders, based on Psalm 68:11,
"The Lord gave the word and great was the company of those who published it."

Cover design by Joel Uber
Interior design by Jomar Ouano

Published in the United States of America

ISBN: 978-1-62024-691-7
1. Biography & Autobiography / Educators
2. Biography & Autobiography / Adventurers & Explorers
13.07.01

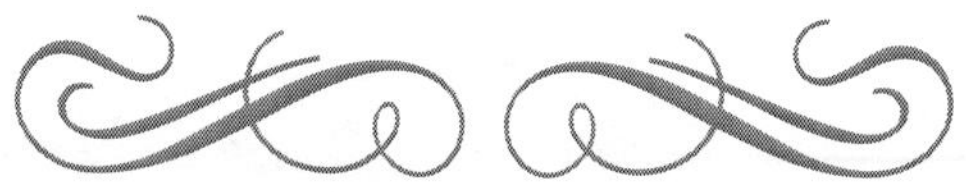

Dedication

To

Kit Carter, my sister, who shared pre-memory years in China with me and provided suggestions to our mother in the preparation of this manuscript.

And

Our parents, Ralph and Elizabeth,
With love

Contents

Foreword 15

PART 1

New Day in China 19
Riding the Tiger 29
Brink of the World 35
The Unknown Begins 39
War by Propaganda 49
"Mrs. Born Before" 59
Charcoal Smoke 63
Broken Threads 69
Down With…! 75
The Clock Strikes 81
Quivering Web 93
The Shattered Wall 99

PART II

Return 107
The Battle 115
Dragon Dance 133

Walls ---141
The College Burns------------------------------------151
Baby and a Bamboo Chair ----------------------------175
Precious Jade ---197
E-song and the Law ---------------------------------201
Ding-chung—Magic Worker ------------------------211

PART III

The Key ---225
Canopy of Heaven -----------------------------------237
Bandits --251
Students ---255
The Conferences ------------------------------------269
Su-sieng ---279
The Party---293
Hope Can Warm a Man -----------------------------303
Shou Hsing Gung -----------------------------------315

Acknowledgements ---------------------------------331

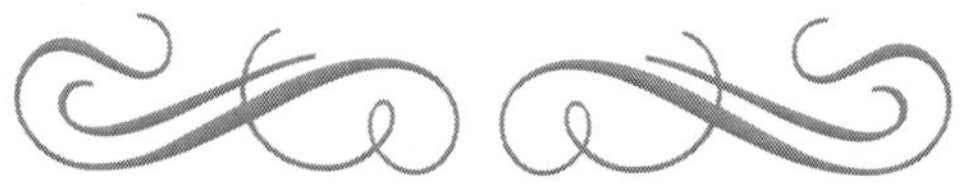

ILLUSTRATIONS

Map of Southeastern China------------------------165

Map of Foochow environs ------------------------166

White Pagoda ------------------------------------167

White Pagoda Seen through our Front Door -------168

Our House in Foochow ----------------------------169

Gunboat on the Min River-------------------------169

Sampan on the Min River -------------------------170

Bamboo Chair--------------------------------------170

Students with Ralph -------------------------------171

Whitney, Ka-trine, and Myself--------------------171

Farewell Card-Obverse ---------------------------172

Farewell Card- Reverse ---------------------------173

Shou Hsing Gung ---------------------------------173

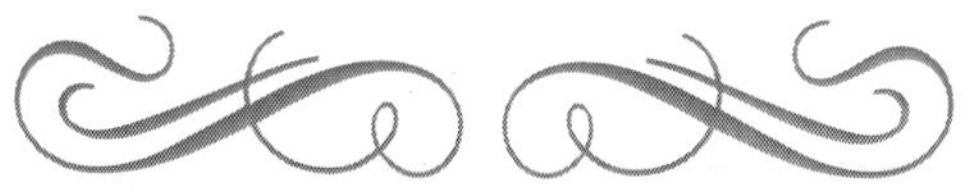

Foreword

My parents were sent to China in 1926 to be educators at Foochow College by the American Board of Commissioners for Foreign Missions (ABCFM). This is my mother's story of their experiences as recorded in a draft manuscript before she passed away in 1976. I have edited her manuscript and know she would be plcased.

—William Whitney Shrader,
Stow, Massachusetts 2011

Part 1

New Day in China

December 1926

We had travelled—by train, ocean steamer, coastal steamer, river launch, sampan, and finally rickshaw—to the ancient walled city of Foochow, China. (Modern name Fuzhou)

And now, late fall of 1926, a few weeks after our arrival, the city of Foochow waited—fearfully, hopefully.

Within the city, *we* waited—my husband Ralph, and I.

Rumors. Many rumors.

An army was on the way!

In China an invading army always brought terror. But this army, in the fall of 1926, was different. The soldiers were well disciplined, the rumors said. How could that be? Soldiers always took what they wanted.

No, this time it was different. This army, under its new young leader, Chiang Kai-shek, brought hope of better times.

Well, some said, wait and see. Look out for your merchandise though. And your women. Board up your shops. Don't trust an army.

Ralph and I were only vaguely disturbed by the rumors. Newly arrived from America and living in insulated security in a walled compound in the middle of the ancient city, we scarcely knew what was happening. A change of regime fitted well into the pattern of the China we had read about. It wouldn't affect us personally, we thought. We were studying the Foochow dialect hours every day preparing eagerly to teach at Foochow College in another compound across the wall from us. However, as the threatening rumors grew, my too vivid imagination painted frightening pictures. Would there be fighting in the streets? Would we be forced to flee this exciting city before we started to attain our long-held dream? Before we had more than glimpsed the college we had come to serve? Facts were elusive.

It was the first week of December. Tension hung in the air like a too-tight elastic. Then, suddenly on a cold clear morning, the moment we had feared was here. An order was issued—no one would be permitted on the streets. The Nationalist (Southern) Army was approaching the outskirts of the city, and the Northern soldiers fleeing Foochow were "catching coolies" to serve as load bearers. Ah, now we understood. That was why the servants had not gone shopping this day!

More rumors. And a thousand questions.

What would happen now? Was the young revolutionary leader we had heard about, Chiang Kai-shek, personally in command of the army which had come marching out of Canton (Modern name Guangzhou) to unify China? Yes, some said. No, said others. Was his army Communist?

No... Yes... Wait and see.

Ralph and I along with the rest had to wait and see.

Of course we had known China was on the verge of upheaval before we left the states. That was routine. And we had lived with the rumors about this new army for some weeks. Even as our ship had plowed west across the Pacific during the past summer, daily shipboard bulletins kept us informed, until Chiang Kai-shek's name rolled easily off everyone's tongue. American gunboats were bombed on the Yangtze River. What did that portend? Would we be allowed to land in Shanghai? Oh, yes. Shanghai was the West. Shanghai was safe. There would always be a Shanghai!

But there was threat in the air, and the new army was marching north.

The rumors greeted us on the waterfront when we arrived in Foochow on October first in the person of soldiers who stopped us to examine our baggage. With bayonet guns over their shoulders and hand grenades dangling from too twitchy fingers they explained, "The Nationalist Army is getting closer every day."

Contradictory rumors of their progress persisted as we started language class and continued our China studies through October and November.

And now, on this December day, the army was at our gates. We would see for ourselves what would happen.

Until late in the afternoon, Ralph and I, with Gertrude and Arthur Rinden who had traveled to China with us, tried to concentrate on Chinese phrases. Our Chinese teachers seemed distracted but told us nothing. When they left, early, we went cautiously to the street just outside our compound to reconnoiter. From a woman pulling her child into her shop, and gathering up long strands of drying noodles, we heard more rumors—someone had found kerosene soaked cotton waste stowed in vulnerable spots. Fire? A wood-constructed city in flames? I shivered!

How ominous the unusual silence of the streets in this afternoon hour—no traffic, not a rickshaw, no policeman, no soldiers—just silence that forebode. The children, even the ragged dogs, had been taken within the closed shop fronts that stared back at us warningly. Occasionally a man would stick his head through the last open slit of his doorway and peer up and down the deserted street, then push his final board into place. We could hear the bar slide across inside. Keep out, it said, filling the empty street, and me, with fear. Go home.

We returned to our compound. The old timers were not talking. Leonard and Agnes Christian, our temporary host and hostess, greeted us with shrugs, and an aura of calm waiting.

Dinner was tense. The house-boy, in his patched short-coat and wide cotton trousers, put a platter of tasteless beef before Mr. Christian, who said, "Well, I see Li-guang was able to get us some meat. Beef's gone up."

At first we tried to pretend that everything was normal. Conversation stepped carefully around the situation. The Christians, like most of the old timers, were for the old regime of the North—more stable, they said. Our sympathy was with Chiang Kai-shek's young Nationalists from the South. Already there had been skirmishes between the two armies in some outlying villages, and Ralph, Arthur, and Neil Lewis had been asked to go out and help pick up wounded soldiers and bring them to our hospital. Alice Lewis, wife of our Doctor Neil, Gertrude, and I had felt heroic sewing Red Cross armbands to mark our men as rescuers. They had come home excited and depressed with stories of the wounded men they had brought in.

Now, with the army outside our city walls, I had to break through my fear of the unknown. "But what may happen?"

Mrs. Christian, straight-lipped, answered, "No one knows what is going to happen."

"But what are the possibilities? I'd like to know the worst."

Mr. Christian, always so ready to joke, did not smile. "When a Chinese city changes hands nothing may happen. Or anything."

"What is the worst?" I persisted. Ralph frowned at me.

Mr. Christian laughed. "So you'll know what you missed if it doesn't happen?"

"That's about it."

"Well, then. Looting. Possibly fighting in the streets."

"But they wouldn't come in here? Fight us?" My stomach began to hurt.

I looked at Ralph eating as if armies came in every day. So, he was trying to tell me—what's a little coup d'état?

"Usually they don't bother the foreigners," said Mr. Christian cheerfully. "But in this case the Nationalist Army has its left wing advisors. Borodin, you've heard of him, a Communist trained in Moscow, is in charge of propaganda. No one knows."

There was silence.

The Christians had been in China a long time. Mr. Christian had entered Peking with the American armed forces during the Boxer rebellion at the turn of the century. [The Boxer Rebellion resulted in the deaths of hundreds of missionaries and tens of thousands Chinese Christians.]

I knew there was much unsaid.

It was night. The army was still waiting outside the city wall.

Our men took their turns at guard duty inside the compound. Through the quiet cold, they paced, two on a shift, their heels clicking on the stone walks. The city lay below in complete darkness. And silence. No dogs barking, no firecrackers. Not a sound. It was a city of fear and waiting. *I* was afraid…waiting…Ralph was asleep, waiting his turn to be called.

At two o'clock I heard a voice call softly from below our window. "Ralph, Ralph, are you awake? Your turn."

I punched him. "Wake up. It's your turn to go on duty."

He crawled out from under the mosquito net. "Be right down, Neil."

He pulled on his shoes and topcoat. "Bye," he said softly. "Don't worry."

"I won't," I said, lying.

His steps sounded outside and died away. For hours I lay stiff and aching, straining for sounds that never came…

In the morning I awoke to a gorgeous sun. There was Ralph, sleeping again. I had not heard him come in. So nothing had happened. Of course. How natural. Nothing can happen to *us*.

From the lane came the familiar call of the bean cake vender, "Bean cakes, white bean cakes, yellow bean cakes, ahhh!" What music!

Yes, and there were rickshaw horns blaring as usual from the distant street. Life going on as it should. So it was over. And we are still alive. How like China. We'd soon get used to it.

After breakfast, Ralph and I rushed to South Street. It was like a feast day. An arch for flowers was being erected across this main thoroughfare. We asked questions.

The Nationalists had won without a battle. From every shop hung the new flag—a blue flag with a white sun. The old five bars were gone. The rising sun of a new day, people told us. Why, they must have been ready—all these paper flags! Prepared secretly in advance. So the city must have been won long before the army arrived, but no one had dared breathe a word. Sometime during that long night papers had been signed? Money exchanged? Rumors—who could tell? And the Northern Army had slipped quietly away.

The New Day! Huge posters decorated the walls: "The Party's Three Principles: Government of People, for People, by People." *How familiar*, I thought. Most were in Chinese, a few in English.

Through the streets, we saw young men thrusting rice paper notices into outstretched hands. We read, "Eight-hour day. Equal rights for women. Education for all." How like home. "No more opium." Wonderful, that was what China needed. And these next slogans: "Down with militarism! Down with Capitalism! Down with foreign Imperialism!" Well, that had nothing to do with us! So we thought.

Ralph stuffed some of the leaflets into his pocket.

That night under the flower arches the city held a great welcoming parade. We pressed through the crowd and climbed up on a low wall from where we watched the marchers—all the thousand-year-old guilds, new fashioned into labor unions, each under the brilliant swaying lanterns of its individual trade. As they marched, the lanterns lighting their faces, they sang their revolutionary song, again and again, like a round…it reminded me of *Scotland's Burning*.

The words were foreign to us, but the music familiar. And how exciting the brightness of their eyes and the release of their spirits. The crowd took up the song—a great rousing triumphant song that shouted aloud the arrival of the New Day. Let them not be disappointed, my heart cried.

So we saw the Nationalist Party with flags flying, lanterns glowing, many young voices singing, bring the New Day to Foochow. And we were in the midst. History swirled around us and leaped ahead of us. We sensed its drive, its elemental power, its potential for good or evil—a force that had been gathering for decades—far too big for us to touch, or bend, or shape…

Stirred by what we saw, but with a sense of foreboding, we could only ask, are we too late? Is America too late? *Is the West too late?*

We joined in the singing.

Almost, we believed with them in the New Day!

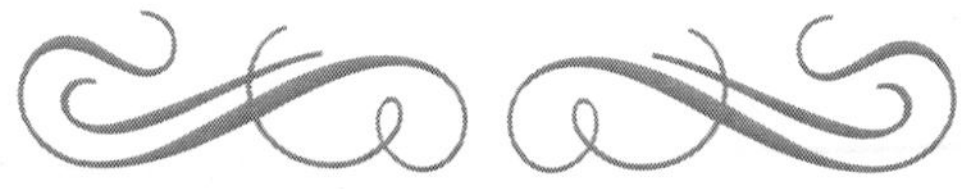

Riding the Tiger

Flashback to College

Later that night, after the parade, in the small upstairs bedroom in the Christians' home, I could not sleep. The New Day was too exciting. Filled with hope? Yes. But what else? What would be my role in it? Ralph's?

In language class we had learned that Chinese proverb, "He who rides a tiger cannot dismount." Had my husband and I unwittingly mounted a tiger? Could we ride it? I looked at him beside me—so strong and unafraid.

But I wondered.

While he slept peacefully, I thought about our dream—no, our goal.

It had been clearly defined for years. Ralph and I wanted to go to China to work with students—not just to teach, but to learn from them—to share with them. We shaped our graduate studies to that end, Ralph taking his Bachelor of Divinity at Chicago Theological Seminary, and both taking courses at the University of Chicago.

But when I tried to explain to curious friends what motivated us, I was confused. There was the war, the world, China, hunger, God, shouting Chinese students, our lives—all mixed up.

There was the slaughter in Europe we had both lived through, and Jesus saying, "I came that they might have life."

It was a most impractical dream, we knew, impelling us to go abroad when most Americans were only too happy to be in America, making their safety doubly sure by erecting those post–World War One walls of isolationism about us.

We were being stubbornly nonconformist. Some of our friends even said, "You're crazy. Why should you two bury yourselves out there?"

For Ralph, a decision once made was made. For me it continued to be debatable. On one thing, through the three years of our studies, we agreed—we would go to China. We would go to work with students. Always it was the students.

At the university we took such courses as we could on China—its history, culture, art, particularly the current problems—all the more fascinating because we would soon be there to see for ourselves. Conversations between us occurred daily. Now I reviewed them.

"Ralph, I can't explain logically to our friends why we want to go. It would be much simpler if we were doctors."

Ralph smiled at me patiently as he always did when I was floundering. "Educators are doctors, in their way.

But it's really very simple. For me it's a compulsion. "Call it a 'call.'"

"But you can't call it a 'call' today. Not at the university. That's too unscientific."

Ralph continued, "It depends on what you mean by a 'call.'" He countered, "Why do you want to go?"

I grinned at him. "You know, you idiot!"

"No, that won't do. You want to go as much as I do. It's mutual."

"All right, it's mutual. But why? What ever started us?

We were silent awhile as we both reached back. He said, "There was John R. Mott, the great internationalist. And Sherwood Eddy...at Estes Park."

"Yes, we were both at that conference at Estes Park, don't forget. There was that pine tree and the moonlight on the mountain peaks, and..."

"There was Sherwood Eddy who had visited Russia and was telling about China—the sleeping dragon that was waking up and would shake the world. China—what a mess the white man had made out there. And we are supposed to 'have God' and be a 'Christian country'!"

"I remember the terrible famines he talked about and the revolution and the students."

"That's it—the students—the importance of helping them become world-minded leaders. You know—'the war to end war.'"

We paused to reach further back. I repeated, "*World* minded. The war had something to do with it. What happened to you in France?"

Ralph didn't like to talk about this. The first time was in college one day when we were riding in his Model T in the rain, and had to button on the side curtains. In spite of the curtains, I shivered as he pictured the night he felt the earth shaking from the big guns. St. Mihiel sector. Finally the men returned to their dugouts through a long low valley dense in fog. In the morning Ralph's face was swollen, his eyes matted and temporarily blind. Chlorine gas had lain heavy in that fog. He with others was taken to a base hospital where, convalescing, he wrote letters for men who didn't want their wives or mothers to know how badly off they were.

He said, "I'll never forget their bloated faces, or how they tried to make their letters cheerful. Sometimes a man would die in the midst of a letter. When you see men die, your buddies, something of you goes with them. And something of them stays with you. 'Why?' you ask. 'What's it all about?' And the next question is, 'What can I do about it?'"

I had experienced the war, too, from a distance. My older cousins had been in France. Battle headlines were my morning and evening diet. Now, as we planned our future, I said, "What does this have to do with our going to China?"

Ralph said, "I've seen what hate can do. Now I'd like to see what love—call it purposeful goodwill—can do."

He paused, and I saw in his eyes the stubborn look that France had given him. "The war turned my religion inside out. I have to *do* something about it. Not just personal salvation—something related to the world. We—the nations—must begin to try to understand each other. To survive. We have to find a meeting ground in the no-man's-land of hatreds and fears…"

I said, "I want to go to discover."

"Discover what?"

"I don't know for sure. Simply as a woman—to see if we can get through—make friends with people who have been calling white men 'foreign devils' for a century. With reason, of course. People noted for their courtesy and culture. And to see if there is a way to relieve the massive human misery we've heard about. I know neither of us is going to China to snatch souls from a hot hell, Buddhist or Christian. Not the old motive—salvation."

Ralph said, "The students are throwing out their old religions. As educators you are constantly redefining 'salvation.' You must help them reinterpret the old terms into spiritual values which can have meaning to them in their modern technological world. Salvation—wholeness—highest possible fulfillment. That could include salvation for this munitions mad world, too."

"There is another thing. I don't like being called a 'missionary.' It makes me sound so much better than I am. I can't stand pious people."

The twinkle in Ralph's eyes reminded me that no one could accuse him of piosity. "You certainly don't look like one." He brushed his hand over my recent "windblown" bob. "The unfortunate connotation—the too pious image—doesn't really matter. It's what you put into the word. It is really a great word."

Our congregational board had offered us a choice between Foochow College in China and an opening in the Philippines. We had been reading articles about "China's New Day—Revolution or Renaissance?" The control of the Western powers was breaking down, with a rise to power of the East. Students of the middle schools and colleges, influenced by intellectuals like Hu Shih, were in the vanguard of this movement.

Ralph said, "The Chinese students are on the move. Working with them we'll be working with the stream of history."

"It could be very exciting!"

We said to the board, "China...China, of course!"

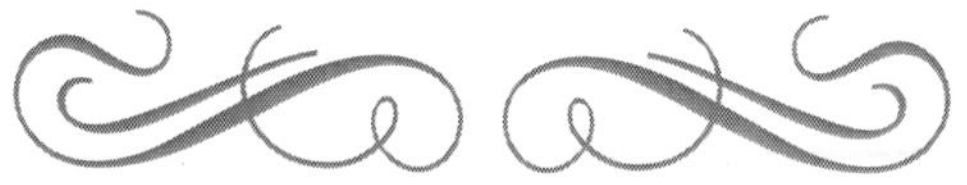

Brink of the World

Flashback to Ship—Fall 1926

Our New Day? What about the home and family we planned to have? Back in Chicago our dream had been so alluring. *Already it is changing into a thousand question marks*, I thought, as I gazed out at the White Pagoda casting its moon bright shadow across our compound wall and the tennis court below. Against this peaceful scene flashed a poster I had noticed during the parade that afternoon, one with a caption in English: "Down with Capitalism! Down with Foreign Imperialism!" Did that mean us? No. We aren't imperialists. We're here to be friends. Surely we will be allowed to live in peace—to have our home. Or will we? Will we experience defeat or compromise?

I wondered, like a little girl who wanted to run across the hall to my mother's room for comfort, and a shot of her staunch courage.

I wondered, remembering a day on shipboard when Gertrude and I were talking. She and Arthur, like Ralph and me, were facing a new life in China.

Indulging for a moment in the romance of Chinese legends and travel folders, I had said, "What do you think it will be like? Marble moon bridges and pagodas with tinkling bells?"

"More likely, enormous sows with unbelievable litters. In the front room, I've heard tell."

"Gertrude! What are you planning to do? Teach? Or be a model housewife?"

"Probably a smattering of both." She sighed. "Both badly."

Gertrude was sewing up a white dress from some silk she had bought in Shanghai. The small coastal steamer plowed south toward Foochow, nearer and nearer to the unknown. After weeks of up rootedness, of land and sea travel, I longed for a home. But how dream of a home when an army is marching north? I thought this and guessed Gertrude was thinking it too. But we didn't say it. We wanted to forget fear.

"Arthur wants to work in the country, Ingtai, very close to the people. I am trying not to envy you living in the city at Foochow College."

I guessed she was thinking of that very crowded deck below us packed with deck passengers, children, bundles and baskets. Chickens. The enormous but emaciated sow we had seen.

We glanced at our two husbands so eager, so absorbed.

"What do you do if you have a baby?" Gertrude asked. "Did you bring things or trust to Foochow?"

"Trusted to Foochow. I suppose they have babies there."

"Ummm, I suppose so. Lots of them. But…" I recalled the absence of clothing on most of them on the deck below.

"Anyway," I asked, "what do you think they'll be like?"

"The Americans?" Gertrude regarded the dress in her lap. "Probably all saints. Saints under queer hats."

Living with saints for six years, or maybe life—appalling!

"I'm glad you're along."

She stood up and held the dress in front of her.

"It looks grand," I said enviously.

"It's awfully short. Do you suppose they'll approve? They told us they were looking forward to seeing the new styles."

"Are you afraid of them?"

"Terribly, but don't tell Arthur. Look." She pointed to the horizon. "I feel like Columbus about to fall off the brink of the world."

The next morning, in a frenzy of suitcases, we had only porthole glimpses of low, rugged mountains as our boat passed the island of Matsu and, rounding Sharp Peak island, headed up the Min River. Arthur and Ralph had disappeared to struggle with the larger baggage problem. Gertrude burst into our cabin. "We're there!"

The place to get off…the brink of the world…where the unknown begins…

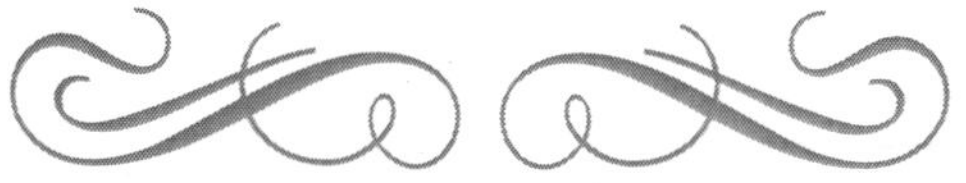

The Unknown Begins

Flashback to Fall 1926

At Pagoda Landing the Seikyo stopped, its anchor chain clanging against the side of the boat. To me there was finality about it. Well, you're here. You wanted a big adventure. Now you've got it, and you can't get out of it for years and years!

Here, where the Min River widened to a natural harbor, the coastal steamers stopped for customs and quarantine inspection. A cluster of junks, their square sterns painted in brilliant dragon designs, lay at anchor close by.

You're here! That's all that seemed clear to me.

Our steamer was instantly surrounded by small riverboats. We watched from our upper deck as shouting boat men leaped the railings below, pulled the deck passengers into their sampans, and tossed off the Chinese baskets including the chickens and the sow. I heard the strange jabbering language. Terrifying madhouse. And the quiet insistence inside of me—you're here and you can't get out of it. My heart pounded. The wind blew hard, and the sampans bumped each other on the bouncing waves.

At last a river launch pushed its way between the Chinese boats to the side of our ship, and we saw a group of Americans waving, smiling at us, beckoning to us. Americans! We climbed down the swaying steps, hanging fiercely to the rope rail, and jumped into the plunging launch. The wind blew hard against us as our little boat pulled from the side of the steamer. Now the watery space was too big to leap across. Now too wide to call across. It was breaking the last connection with home. The steamer would go back to Shanghai. We were going ahead to the city—the city called Hok-cieu, Valley of Happiness.

Gertrude and I sat on the roof of the small cabin battling the wind as it caught and blew high our "flapper" skirts. The people in China hadn't seen modern styles for a long time. The two men and three women who had come to meet us sat on camp stools in the prow facing us, the men hanging onto their sun helmets. One woman wore a queer hat—but she didn't look like a saint. Their faces were lined but excited too. Wisps of gray hair came loose and blew in the wind. The little boat jumped with the waves and vibrated with the loud noise of its engines. We couldn't hear what anyone said.

They examined us curiously…our bobbed hair. Such short hair! And the style they had anticipated having their native tailors copy! Were we disappointing them?

Our two husbands leaned against the rail, Arthur holding his new white sun helmet in his hand. The sun struck his head. "You'd better put it on!" shouted Mr. Christian.

Tawny sails of river junks drifted down on the out-rushing current to meet and pass us.

"What's the latest slang?" called Dr. Beard, senior of the group and president of Foochow College.

"Listen to Arthur awhile and you'll know," said Gertrude.

The wind grew boisterous. Mr. Leger moved to the sheltered side of the cabin.

"He's our genius," said Mr. Christian. "He did three years of language in one year, and now he's writing a Foochow dictionary. He'll be your boss in language lessons. You'll begin tomorrow." I had noticed Mr. Leger's thin scholarly face. But language study—tomorrow! Well, they wasted no time here!

We rounded a point. Mr. Christian shouted above the wind. "Look! Now you can see the White Pagoda. There!" Whitecaps lashed the boat and sprayed us with their cool drops. Through the spray we saw the distant blur of a city miles ahead. And the pagoda, a mere speck against the sky.

"It shows us where home is. It's just outside the compound wall. Built before William the Conqueror.

"What?" seemed to say the faces of these people who had taken a whole day off to welcome us. "These young things? They have come to help us?"

At last we anchored below the Bridge of Ten Thousand Ages, an ancient mile-long stone span uniting the sprawling city. Sampans surrounded us, their women screaming for trade. Like the prey of vultures we were pulled into separate boats, bags crunching in after us. Ralph? Where was Ralph? I spotted him being rowed off in another sampan. But here was Dr. Beard beside me giving instructions in an easy flow of Chinese. Two river women, blue trousers rolled to their thighs, poled a heavy oar. The current, swift and angry, fought for us.

Miraculously we reached the shore. Mr. Christian leaped ahead and pulled us one by one up a narrow board to the bank. Rickshaw pullers surrounded us shouting. And all about our heads I heard that strange language flying—like a flock of excited birds.

Mr. Christian, agile, strong, assured, was everywhere at once, issuing orders like a king. Why, he was laughing! Quickly he had us each in a rickshaw and on our way.

At the head of the Bridge of Ten Thousand Ages we were stopped by a group of curt uniformed soldiers.

"What's the idea?" Ralph called.

"Martial law, they're looking for firearms," said Dr. Beard. "They say the Nationalist Army is getting closer every day."

That army again, I thought, annoyed.

Mr. Christian pulled out calling cards and distributed them to the bayoneted soldiers who inspected them and motioned us to pass. An officer, halting us, pointed to Ralph who was carrying the radio he had made from blueprints and cherished all the way from America. A guard started to take it from him. I saw Ralph's stricken look as Dr. Beard protested. Close beside us a grim faced guard dangled a hand grenade and my skin prickled.

A rapid exchange in Chinese. "You'll have to get a permit," Dr. Beard said to Ralph. "Come with me, we'll have to see the top authorities." And with misgivings I saw the two of them turn back toward the bridge.

We moved ahead toward the walled city through a narrow, crowded street with bewildering Chinese signs.

Rickshaws lurched. Horns blared. Chinese men and women walked indifferently in front of us, beside us, behind us. Coolies shouted. Enormous loads swayed from poles on the shoulders of sweating men. Slippery fish glistened in baskets. Shining brass objects hung in shop stalls.

I felt in a dream—Marco Polo. *I'm the stranger. Lost. Where am I? Is this real? Are they real?* Then in a shop front, I glimpsed a small boy clutching his father around the neck and weeping aloud. And farther on, a girl with shiny black hair kicking a shuttle cock, and her laughter reached me through the din. *Why, they* are *real—they are just like us!* It was no longer so strange. Out of all the people I saw those children. My heart lifted. And they were gone. *Later…later…* I thought.

After three miles our rickshaws passed under the massive arched entrance of the old city wall, turned into a quiet lane and stopped before a wooden gate in a low white wall. To our right the White Pagoda towered above us.

"This is Peace Street," Mr. Christian said. The gate opened, and we saw a line of servants coming out to welcome us. They threw strings of firecrackers to the ground and I held my hands to my ears as they banged around us. Peace Street? A giant cracker burst at my feet.

"*Bing-ang, bing-ang* (peace, peace)!" the servants shouted and bowed, smiling and shaking their own hands in their wide sleeves.

A wrinkled gateman held the door wide, pleasure creasing his eyes, and we climbed a flight of stone steps leading up to our walled compound. Green lawns, trees, flowers. And well apart, several solid brick houses with arched verandahs hidden behind palms and tropical shrubs. After the alien street, here indeed was peace on a rising hill!

Gertrude and Arthur went up to the doctor's home where they were to stay. Ralph and I were to live at the Christians' until we could keep house.

It was late afternoon, and I was beginning to worry, when Ralph arrived with his radio. He showed me a document covered with black characters and red seals.

"This is a permit. We should frame it. I have met all the high officials of Foochow."

I patted the radio. "How did you get it?"

"Drank tea. Cups of tea. With each one. Trouble," they said. "These new fangled foreign things—how do we know you won't be using it to communicate with the enemy?" And each sent me on to the next higher. When we got to the top, he didn't have anyone higher to consult.

Dr. Beard assured him it was harmless so he stamped the permit. We belong.

The sun set behind mountains and a distant black pagoda. The hot wind stopped blowing. Bugle calls, minor and off-key, came from city walls, crisscrossing the city from all directions—a golden net of sound. Call and answer, call and answer. Friend? Enemy? Who was the enemy?

That sultry evening I sat on the edge of our bed in the little upstairs room and, with borrowed needle and thread, let down the first dress I could pull out of my suitcase.

Ralph was busy. He could not wait to install his radio—this miracle thing he had carried so carefully halfway around the world. He would command, "Hold this wire," or "Run downstairs and catch this when I throw it out to you."

He was stringing a new copper aerial to the banyan tree and dropping a wire to a grounded pipe. The four Leger children assisted, climbing the banyan tree and relaying the news to several households. Come and see.

They could not yet believe in this new marvel. Voices—music—by airwaves? All the way from Shanghai or Hong Kong? Breathlessly and on tiptoe all the Americans in the compound slipped into the small, hot bedroom, afraid to disturb the conjuror or his magic box.

The air was still—they wiped their faces. I invited them to sit on the bed. Ralph strode out for a tool. Something wasn't working, I could tell by the tight look around his eyes. The Chinese amah came in to lower the bed mosquito net and backed out mystified. We waited as ordinary mortals wait the final test of a scientist's invention. At last the tubes lighted. Ralph plugged in the two pairs of headphones and beckoned to me. We put them on. How expectant our audience looked. Then fearful. Sounds by air? How could airwaves possibly find Foochow, so isolated from the world? And what kind of sounds would there be in this far strange country? Then through the static, I heard a familiar beat. Rhythm. It cleared. Words? We've got it? Shanghai broadcasting. Music—there it is—music, loud in our earphones. Familiar. A favorite American tune. Incredible—the irony of it! "Show me the way to go home. I'm tired, and I want to go to bed!" Ralph and I laughed aloud.

One by one our guests took their turns at the headphones. One by one their rapt faces relaxed into smiles. We were linked with the world. A new day was born for them in Foochow.

I recalled so clearly that first night in the little room with the old-fashioned casement windows, while Ralph slept and I suffocated in the breathless heat. Tonight, the misty white mosquito net hung down enfolding us, hemming us terribly and finally in.

As tonight, I crawled from under the net and went to the window. There was the White Pagoda, gleaming in the hot moonlight, too still, too calm. Night sounds of a disturbing strangeness drifted up from the lane outside the wall. A temple gong from the hill above boomed with slow then rapid beat. That first night I had heard for the first time the now comforting hollow-bamboo rattle of the night watchman making his rounds. And I noticed some unidentified sounds—clicking, clattering sounds, with at intervals a clattering crash. Vaguely they recalled something—chattering—sparrows—Mah Jong, a gambling game. That was it. A Mah Jong game was being played in a house just outside our wall. Building the wall of ivory chips, the rapid sharp game, then breaking it down, crash! Over and over. I lay awake that first night and many nights thereafter, waiting for the crashing sounds outside our wall.

Now on this New Day I knew our city wall had not crashed. It had opened! But to what? To friend or enemy? To destruction...or to the realization of our dreams?

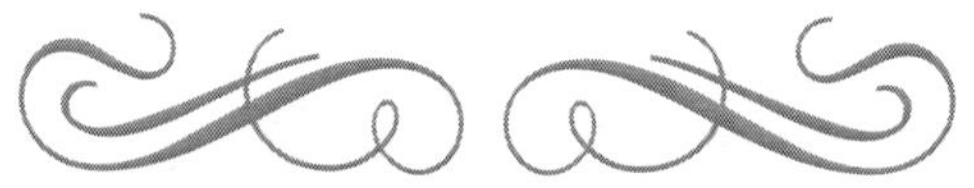

War by Propaganda

December 1926

The remainder of that night following the parade I slept fitfully and then was rudely awakened by a smiling Ralph dressed and ready for breakfast. I said, "What time is it?"

"Time enough for you to dress."

When I came into the dining room, I found Ralph studying the leaflets that had been thrust into his hands during the parade the night before. Mr. Christian was glancing down the columns of characters. Except for a few English phrases, these were not translated. I started to hand them on to someone else but Ralph had said, "I'm curious." So here they were.

But the sun was shining, and I was feeling the giddy lightness of relief from the tension of the past days. I said, "Well, it's over—we've seen the revolution come and conquer without firing a shot."

"Scarcely a shot," Ralph corrected me.

"So far," said Mr. Christian, and my high spirits tumbled.

"What do you mean? Didn't the city change hands and no trouble?"

Mr. Christian shrugged. "In China we foreigners can live in the middle of a situation and not really know what is going on. Of course, a lot of the Chinese don't know either."

"But you read Chinese?" I pointed to the yellow sheets.

"Oh, that. That's propaganda. The Chinese in Canton (modern name Guangzhou) are having an expert help right now. There's a lot of Communism mixed up in this. We've heard they've been making things tough for the foreigners down there—trying to drive them out by harassment—not letting the servants work for them, burning their buildings, and so on. No, a revolution that's been building for over a century isn't won in a night."

I was full of wishful thinking. "Everyone looked so happy. And all the promises…"

Mr. Christian rose. "I have to go now to a meeting at the consulate. Maybe I can find out where we stand. Why don't you take these up to your language teacher to translate for you? You may find them interesting." He handed the yellow sheets to Ralph and left.

So on the first morning of Foochow's New Day, we went eagerly to class taking the rice paper documents with us. Iong Sinang said, "I cannot speak your language. Take these to Liu Sinang, history teacher at Foochow College."

We suspected that Iong Sinang knew more English than he was allowed to use. Or was this some innate courtesy making him reluctant to tell us what the propagandists were crying out against the foreigners? Later Ralph returned with neatly written translations by Mr. Liu.

The first one:

NOTIFICATION IN MEMORY OF WORKING MEN

Workers! Friends! Dear Workers! Dear Friends!

Recall: Four years ago your working friends of the Peking-Hankow railroad were killed by the northern military general, Wu Pei-fu. This made you see how the working men are being oppressed. You united, arose, and for one day fought for your own benefit. You were, for one day in the history of our revolution, the greatest and most glorious page. Now you must know why your fellow workers were killed by Wu Pei-fu.

All people of China are under the double oppression of militarism and imperialism. All men long to be free of this oppression. The workers were killed because the interests of the people clashed with those of the military. Understand how the military are exploiting you. Organize. Then rule of the militarists will soon be ended.

We cry aloud:

Workers of all the country unite and arise!

Workers of all Fukien Province unite and arise!

Down with Imperialism!

Down with Militarism!

Uphold the Southern Army departing for the North!

Uphold the Peoples' Government!

Fight the North and win forever!

The Peoples' Revolution forever!

China's Peoples' Party forever!

Signed: China's Peoples' Party, Fukien Province

We needed help and summoned Mr. Leger.

Glancing over the translations, he said, "The long tentacles from Moscow! You've heard of the Communist Mikhail Borodin? This is obviously his hand and that of his Russian assistants. Borodin heads the Nationalist Army's Propaganda Department."

"But this isn't propaganda, its truth—the killing of the workers of the railroad, and the double oppression of militarism and imperialism. This has happened," Ralph insisted.

"What do you mean by propaganda?" asked Mr. Leger. "The original intent of the word? To spread a body of knowledge? To inform? Or what it has come to imply—something false or slanted? Is this slanted? Certainly it is truth, but it omits other truths. This is warfare by propaganda. These little rice paper leaflets contain a weapon more powerful than guns."

"But Chiang Kai-shek comes with an army," I said.

"True," said Mr. Leger. "War lords and imperialist nations must be met with their own weapons. But at the moment the Nationalists have very little in the way of arms. Did you notice the new Nationalist flags all over the city yesterday? Foochow was won in advance, by these." He tapped the leaflets.

I was excited. *Look*, I thought, *wasn't time turning a page we should underline in red with exclamation points? Are we seeing for the first time in history Communism reaching out from its European home base to win a foreign country, relying mainly on its potent weapon—Ideas?*

As Mr. Leger talked, I thought fearfully that Ralph and I were caught in this page of history—what of our home? The children we want? Are we to sacrifice these for a Communist dream?

Ralph was saying, "But what about Sun Yat-sen? What is happening to his 'Last Will and Testament' to the people?"

"His cloak has fallen on Chiang Kai-shek. His dream of a democratic government was badly upset when we let him down."

"How do you mean—let him down?"

Now, with the propaganda sheets in our hands, this seemed important. Now it affected our lives.

Mr. Leger continued. "Dr. Sun wanted his government to be a true by-the-people affair. You remember he had studied in Hawaii and the United States. China had been one of our allies in World War I. He needed our help if he was to carry through his plan for a democratic government, so he sent a representative to the American minister in Peking asking for recognition of his government, and abrogation of the 'Unequal Treaties.' [The "unequal treaties" were not treaties because they were not negotiated between the nations. The Western powers imposed the conditions. They forced China to pay large amounts of reparations after wars and open up ports for trade.]

And here is a bit of truth most American's haven't heard—his request was turned down!"

America behind her isolation blinders! This was something we had not read in any American paper. So then?

"Russia had just overthrown her regime of tyranny. Dr. Sun went to Shanghai to meet Russian Ambassador Adolphe Joffre. Joffre promised to secure recognition of Dr. Sun's government and to bring over quickly five hundred Russian military and political organizers to train young Chinese for the coming struggle. Dr. Sun accepted the offer but stuck to his position that his government must be *Nationalist*, not Communist, and must be based on his 'Three Principles of the People.'"

"So it's a sort of hybrid revolution?"

Mr. Leger nodded. "The Communist advisors arrived quickly. Marshall Bluecher heads the military group at Whampoa Military Academy as advisor to Chiang Kai-shek. Michael Borodin the Propaganda Department. This could be a turning point in history."

We turned to a second leaflet:

> Farmers, Workers, Traders, Scholars, Soldiers, Women:
>
> Join together and arise!
>
> Throw down imperialistic principles and the running dogs of the military cliques.
>
> Throw down capitalists, and bad gentry, and dishonest lower officials.
>
> Organize a pure and unselfish government!
>
> Truly practice the Three Principles of the People.

Finish the Peoples' Revolution!

China's Revolutionary Party forever!

"You see," said Mr. Leger, "the cry against corruption. China has reached the end of passive acceptance. You've learned the expression *moh huak* in language class which means 'no method,' 'no help for it,' 'nothing can be done.' And you've heard it a hundred times. In the old thinking, if your lot is a hard one, bear it. When warlords ravage your land, when soldiers pillage and burn, suffer. Begin again; gather a small sum to guard against the next adversity. If famine parches the land, live on dry grass and the bark of trees; sell a daughter, or throw the last-born girl-child into the pit made for this. You've seen one on the road to West Gate. Through the centuries there have been waves of desperation, and dynasties have fallen. Again, in this century there has been so much suffering caused by contending warlords and banditry and corruption that people have been eager to listen to voices promising a new day. China needs unity and a stable government. In the background are the 'intellectuals.' In the spotlight the students are distributing literature, organizing mass meetings. They are the spokesmen for the illiterate masses, and therefore hold real political power."

I recalled Ralph's words, "Working with the students, we'll be working with the stream of history." But which stream?

Mr. Leger continued, "At this point you cannot call this a Communist Revolution, but a Nationalist Revolution using Communist techniques. As you read here, the aims of this new People's Party are twofold: to end exploitation by their own warlords and to end exploitation by the Western powers. China has great pride—she wants to take her place among the powerful nations on a basis of equality."

Ralph said, "If they do this they will have the tools of the West." I recalled how the Western powers with gunboats had forced open the port cities and enforced the "Unequal Treaties" so resented by China.

Mr. Leger, his eyes lighting, handed the papers back to Ralph. "Tools of the West—do you mean its culture or its weapons?"

As we went out to our peaceful compound, with the White Pagoda so close, reflecting the sun from its seven tiers, I recalled the symbol of the scales we had dreamed up while preparing to come to China—a pair of giant-sized Chinese scales balanced precariously over some mysterious finger (the finger of God?). On one side dangled a basket labeled *Ill Will*, in it heaped a mixture of ingredients: enforced opium traffic, "Gunboat Diplomacy," "Unequal Treaties," a sign in a Shanghai park: "No dogs or Chinese allowed." White customs officials collecting Chinese tariffs to pay the cost of the "White Man's Burden." Fortunes built on the bent backs of coolies' cheap labor, and the scalded fingers of children picking silk cocoons from boiling water. America's dumped third-rate movies.

Goodwill was on the other side of the scales. Into this basket went ideas—the better aspects of Western culture and thought. Colleges. Western science as applied in medicine, medical colleges, nurses training. Modern agriculture—a step against hunger. Economic development. Schools. The Bible with its concept of the dignity and worth of an individual man.

As the East and West collided, could the goodwill accruing on this side of the scales possibly balance the long accumulation of distrust, even hatred mounting on the other? In so delicate a balance, could it tip the scales toward a harmonious relationship? Or would the heavy weight on the other side pull everything down in some final crash.

I thought, we are only two ordinary Americans. We aren't naïve enough to think we can "save China" or even stem the unfavorable winds of Westernism. We can only try to understand—a fragile leaf on the scales.

The word crisis in Chinese, we learned, was made up of two ideographs—danger and opportunity. Was this our dangerous opportunity?

"Mrs. Born Before"

Flashback to Fall 1926

I recalled how we took the first step toward the realization of our dreams the morning after our arrival. Ralph had said, "We belong." But we would not properly belong until we received our Chinese names. We would be given these at our first morning language class.

Mr. Leger, who lived next door, appeared while we were at breakfast learning to scoop the soft pulp from the red gold persimmons without touching spoons to the outer skin of the fruit.

Within minutes we had found ourselves in the home of Dr. Lora Dyer. In her large living room, sparsely furnished with locally made wicker chairs, sat the four of us—Gertrude, Arthur, Ralph, and I. At one end were a solid oak table and a blackboard. Here stood Iong Sinang, stolid, commanding, in his long gray Chinese gown. Mr. Leger introduced us.

"He speaks no English," said Mr. Leger. "You can communicate only in Chinese." Mr. Iong's face was as blank and motionless as the wall, and about as reassuring.

He bowed, hands in sleeves. "Sinang," he greeted the men. "Sinaniong." He bowed in turn to Gertrude and me.

Mr. Leger interpreted. "Sinang means teacher. Sinaniong, teacher's wife. Or scholar and scholar's wife. They are titles of respect." Writing the words Sieng-sang on the blackboard, he continued, "In Foochow dialect consonants are elided. Sieng-sang becomes Sinang. Add niong, which means woman, or wife, and you have Sieng-sang-niong, or Sinaniong, as we pronounce it. Teacher's wife."

Rapidly he wrote the Chinese characters below the words. "Now the literal translation: Sieng means before. Sang means born. Or transposing them, 'born before.' And Sieng-sang-niong, 'born before wife' or 'Mrs. Born Before.'"

We did not comprehend implications of the words. "Could you tell us what it means?"

Mr. Leger told us about the origin and development of the Chinese picture writing. "You can't always translate Chinese characters into English with exactness, which makes communication sometimes difficult, especially between our nations. There are so many shades of meaning. The characters are symbols, often with philosophic significance and various interpretations. Like poetry they open doors. 'Born before' suggests someone who is out ahead—not literally in years, but in knowledge, experience, wisdom to impart. These are ancient titles, and they reflect the respect that China has always accorded the teacher, the highest in the social order.

"Now you have the title. You must also have a name. You can't be properly registered without a Chinese name. Ralph, I think we have a good one for you." He smiled at Ralph's six feet hardened by college football and more recent work on the tennis court. Turning to the board he wrote "Choi" and a Chinese character. "The symbol for man standing beside the symbol for mountain, on top of the double earth symbol. Man, earth, and mountain. The Chinese may not think of it as having special meaning. Origins of names are usually forgotten, as with ours. But you think about it. You are a man associated with a mountain rising high above the earth. Strength and vision and oneness with the universe. There is a destiny for you." Ralph glanced at me with his brown-eyed twinkle as he copied the characters in his book. "To the Chinese you will simply be Choi Sinang and you"—Mr. Leger turned to me—"will be Choi Sinaniong."

The Rindens would be "Dung" pronounced "Doong" as in moon.

For the next week, Iong Sinang had us "coo" the seven tones of the Foochow dialect. After that we studied phrases, and I began to catch the musical lilt of this southern language. Everywhere we were greeted "Sinang...Sinaniong." What a singing sound for a mere title.

But every day I was discovering how little I knew.

Title of respect—Mrs. Born Before. I felt much too small and ignorant for such a title. There was so much in this sometimes frightening, always interesting, land that neither Ralph nor I knew or understood. Would we ever? Would we ever really be entitled to "Sinang…Sinaniong?"

And now, in the little upstairs room, looking out on the moonlit pagoda so patient in contrast to the frenzied events of the New Day, I recognized my own impatience. Returning to Ralph's side, I pushed away the fear that we might not be given the opportunity to become worthy of the title.

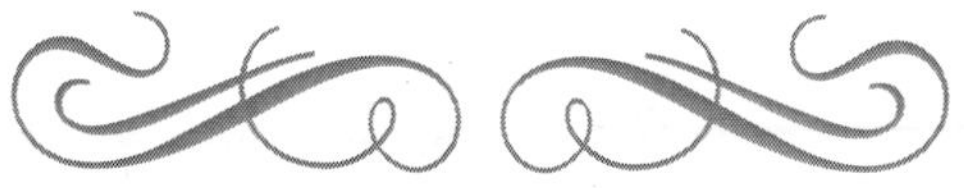

Charcoal Smoke

Winter 1927

In spite of the unsettled conditions, we were going to have a home of our own at last—the house at the top of our hill with screen verandas and spacious rooms. When you looked out through the front door, it made a perfect frame for the White Pagoda.

The walls inside had been washed over with a native yellow calcimine. The floors of rough wide boards had been scraped and covered with sticky Chinese oil that smelled and never dried. Workmen removed the flopping shutters along the screened verandas, mended the broken hooks, and painted the shutters a livid green. They painted by taking a roll of waste cotton, squeezing it in a can of green paint, and with fingers dripping green they rolled this sticky wad back and forth, back and forth, over the old wood. The floors upstairs they painted gray in the same manner, and went over the two twin bathtubs with a flat white. They were going to put the same flat white on the woodwork, but that was too much. I finally produced a sheet of creamy wrapping paper. "Like this," I would try to say in Chinese. "But more yellow. No…this too yellow, I mean." Soon the head man returned with a brilliant mustard yellow sample on a stick. "Moh, moh!" I would exclaim and hunt out another scrap of paper or cloth.

One apprentice perched on a high ladder doing woodwork grinned down at us. Eagerly he followed our progress in the language and with unusual care spoke to us slowly in Chinese.

"*Bing-ang*! (peace-peace). Sinang, Sinaniong," he would sing out to us. "What are you doing?" (A polite phrase.)

"What are you doing?" we would counter in painful syllables.

"Painting house" and the yellow drops would ooze from his fingers dripping to the floor in big round splatters.

"Why don't you use a brush? Do you like to get your fingers covered with paint?"

"We do it this way, Sinaniong, because it is good to do it this way."

A wicker furniture dealer came. We took him around to the other houses showing him chairs, tables and a settee, and ordered thirteen pieces with carefully specified widths and heights. When at last he delivered them, we discovered he had used Chinese inches instead of American. The furniture was all too high. He shrugged. "*Cha-bok-doh* (almost)" literally, short-not-much—an expression we were to hear often! But he took the furniture back and shortened the legs.

Then I hired a cook. I had received much advice on this subject. I had refused several who were too persuasive or shifty eyed. Then Huo Seng came.

"Who's the swell guy with the long silk coat?" asked Mr. Christian, coming in as Huo Seng was leaving.

"My new cook," I said, bursting with pride.

"Scholar and a gentleman for sure. Good recommendations?"

"The best. He cooked for an English family for seventeen years. Here's the letter."

"Reads well," said Mr. Christian.

I couldn't understand his lack of enthusiasm. To me Huo Seng was perfection—tall, gray haired, his kind dark eyes quick to twinkle, and he bore with dignity a pride in his ancient culture.

As a final word, Huo Seng said to me, "You Sinaniong are new in our land, and you will find much that is difficult. I am old and no longer ambitious for great wealth. I will help you, always."

However, the delays were maddening. We were under a strict deadline. We had invited friends over on New year's Day for a house-warming dinner—the young couples, new like us, who had come out within the last year or two: Dr. Neil and Alice Lewis from our compound, Dr. Horace and Mary Campbell up from Pagoda Anchorage, Betty and Mary Cushman from Wenshan Girls' School, and Guy Thelin from the Union Agricultural School. Gertrude and Arthur had gone up the river to Ingtai.

For a whole week, the frantic final preparations had been going on. The floors had dried, almost, our rugs were unrolled, the furniture was put in place. A Chinese rattan bed and plain table with Ningpo varnish stood clean and new in each servant's room. The tin-man had come and on the third trial produced the right size, shape, and number of water cans with spouts and lids so that hot water could be carried to our various brass bowls and tin tubs. The tin tubs leaked, we discovered, and a soldering man had to come. He made long silver streaks across the fresh paint. An electrician finally showed up to poke black rough holes through our freshly calcimined walls for new electric light cords. A carpenter made a kitchen cabinet and, as there were no refrigerators, a screened wind-box to store food. A mason mortared up the large red-tile charcoal-burning cook stove in the smoke blackened kitchen, and the tin smith made a square tin box oven to set over the hot coals for baking our bread. The tailor had finished our bed mosquito nets.

Huo Sang moved in and found a "boy," E-Song, a stocky, pleasant man with a quickness to see and an eagerness to serve. E-Song unpacked the books and arranged them, mostly upside down, in the bookcase. Baskets of charcoal appeared in the kitchen. Water arrived for the large red clay water jars standing in a row on the kitchen veranda. The water came, not through pipes, but in Standard Oil tins swaying from E-Song's carrying pole. It took many trips up the hill from the compound well to fill them.

New Year's Day at last—we were ready to move in! I made the beds—our own sheets on our own beds. E-Song helped. Funny that a strange man should be helping! And I unpacked our clothes into our own bureau drawers. About five o'clock, as I was carrying up the last lot of clothing and entered our front door, I smelled the sweet smoky smell of the charcoal fire drifting down the hall from the kitchen! Then as roasting duck smells followed the smoke I thought, it's *your* food, and pretty soon it will be your own first dinner party with Ralph at the head of your table. You can say what you want and eat what you please. You can go to bed when you choose, and get up when you...well, within reason. Thank goodness. You've had to wait a long time. Come on in and make yourself at home!

Our dinner was perfect—the roast duck and water chestnuts, and steamed English fruit pudding with sauce. Huo Seng, in his long white gown, carved the ducks at a side table. Ralph had refused. I knew he was afraid to do it in front of Huo Seng. The guests were delightful, and I sensed in their lively interest concerning all that was going on about us, the beginning of congenial friendships. I felt as excited as an orphan who has long dreamed of being adopted and wakes up to find herself in a real home.

The spell was still on me when I woke the next morning for the first time in our own sleeping porch. Chinese buglers were practicing their morning bugle calls from distant parts of the city wall, calling back and forth to each other, breaking in, repeating, interrupting, their high minor tunes never ending, not saying anything, just a network of dull brass sound thrown over the waking city. To me they said one thing, "You're in China—and we won't let you forget it, even when you're asleep." Bugle call, bugle call—on and on. But that morning it was a golden sound—there was nothing ominous in it to my ears.

The smell of the sticky Chinese varnish and fresh paint drifted out to me. A good smell. Sounds from the kitchen. Oh, yes, Huo Seng! An honest-to-goodness real live cook! Steps padded down the back veranda and into the bathroom. We heard the plop of a full tin can on the bathroom floor. Hot water. E-Song. Such service. From our beds we could see the temples on the hill cutting their curved silhouettes against the rising sun. Touched with gold, they were.

"Isn't it maddening," said Ralph musingly, "that now that I could sleep late if I wanted to, I don't want to?"

In a few minutes we were taking our first splashes in our own painted tub.

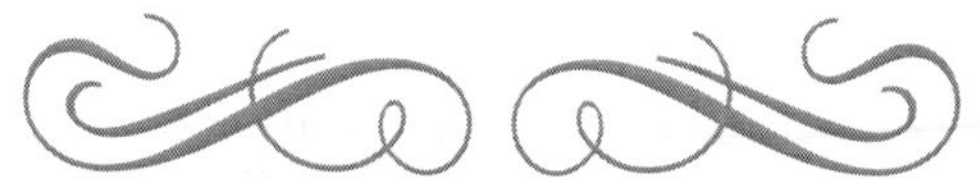

Broken Threads

Winter 1927

For two weeks, life waved its magic wand over us. But someway I knew that twelve o'clock would strike. As old as ecstasy itself must be that ominous nudging against one's heart—this is too good to last.

Home—our own home we had waited for so long—the spacious rooms. The Chippendale bookcase and love seat, all the way from America—and our new wicker mixed incongruously with it. The chairs were hard, but the tailor was going to make cushions when the raw silk arrived from Soochow. The old American style dining set shone with a fresh coat of Ningpo varnish. A large blue flower Japanese batik I tacked up myself over the flower-wood fireplace. There was beauty—the blue of the batik, the blue of the rug, tied by the blue of an antique Chinese bowl.

At the same time, it troubled me. Was this in part a foreign beauty, not belonging here, and would it disappear when the clock struck twelve?

One day this feeling sharpened.

We were at luncheon in our dining room. Suddenly we heard a shuffling of feet on our verandah and looked up expecting to see the grinning face of old Talkie True, a curio man who haunted newcomers until they bought what he wished to sell. But instead were three soldiers, their faces pressed close against the glass panes of the door. They pointed at us and laughed crudely. I noticed on their military caps the white and blue emblems of the Nationalist army, the rising sun. Their cotton uniforms were dirty and the men unkempt. *Had they forced their way through our compound gate?* I wondered.

On our table was meat. They pointed again and shoved each other to get a better view. We sat staring. Then Ralph arose and moved toward the door, on his face a forced smile like a mask, and nodding to them he waved them away with his hand. They pressed harder against the door, no longer laughing. I imagined them bursting in, coming toward us, reaching out…

But it was not yet time for the clock to strike. At that moment E-Song came through the swinging door with a dish of vegetables. He stopped short. Putting down the dish and walking straight to the door he shouted through the glass. In the torrent of angry Chinese, I caught the words, "Go! Americans… Friends… No soldiers allowed here… Go away!"

Slowly they turned and shuffled off the verandah. Then one came back with a last threatening gesture, and his shout came through the door in a strange dialect. I did not know the words. How was it I knew he said, "We will come again!"

We resumed the meal. Then Ralph thought of something. He got up and went to the door to see if it was locked. It was not. So he locked it. I heard the bolt snap into place. It was then that I began to tremble.

What would have happened, I thought, if we had invited them in and with the ancient Chinese courtesy, served them tea and cakes…no, tea and almond cookies?

That evening, a Friday, we packed to go down river for the weekend to Fukien Christian University. Into the big yellow Shanghai suitcase went hiking clothes for a Saturday climb to the top of Kushan Peak, and evening clothes for a dinner party. E-Song went to the gatehouse to call a horse-carriage. When at last it arrived we wedged ourselves into a miniature pumpkin-coach, put the suitcase on our knees, and told the driver "Customs Jetty." From there the university launch would take us the hour's ride down the river.

Our footman, a ragged urchin, gave the small pony a push, a pull, a final shove, and jumped nimbly up behind the carriage. The pony's unshod hoofs clattered on the stones, the sound echoing between the narrow walls of the Chinese homes. We passed a boy making a small fire with idol paper, which burned orange in the dusk. Otherwise the street was deserted. But when we turned onto the main thoroughfare we found ourselves surrounded by a crowd of hurrying people. Fortunately they were moving in the same direction, toward the city gate, and paid us no attention. In the crush we pushed through the arched gate.

Once more the road opened. The crowd was heading toward a definite objective. A short distance down the street we could see the Catholic orphanage behind its low wall. Like a lodestone it was drawing this mob bearing down upon it from all directions. The iron gate had already been broken open, and in horror we watched the crowd pushing up to the barred door and windows. Our pony, caught in the crush of running people, stopped. Our footman jumped to the ground, grabbed the pony's bit and dragged at it. We heard the crash of stone on wood, a loud splintering, and a monster roar from the people. Now the crowd in the street surged toward the orphanage leaving an open space about our carriage, and our footman pulled the pony forward. The driver beat savagely with his whip. We crawled ahead, the boy jerking the pony to the right, to the left, making our opening as we went. We, breathless within the carriage, pushed too with every muscle, silently. Helpless to stem that mob whose anger had been turned against the foreigner, we had only one desire—to remain unseen.

The crowd thinned, the driver shook his whip, the urchin jumped up behind, and the pony gathered momentum and settled into a gentle lope down the street.

All the way I kept wondering about the orphans and sisters. Had they been warned in time to flee? I knew that every compound had a secret escape door hidden in its wall.

At last we saw the Big Bridge and the lights of sampans on the water, a city of sampans. Friendly river—the way to safety.

On the dock at the university, our host and hostess welcomed us. We told them what had happened but did not want to appear too upset, as if we were new to China.

Dr. Scott made light of it, to reassure us, I supposed. "These things happen now and then. After all, this is China. What can you expect?"

The next day no word of trouble reached us at the university. So it had been just another minor incident. We climbed Kushan Peak, and on Sunday afternoon took the launch back up river to the city.

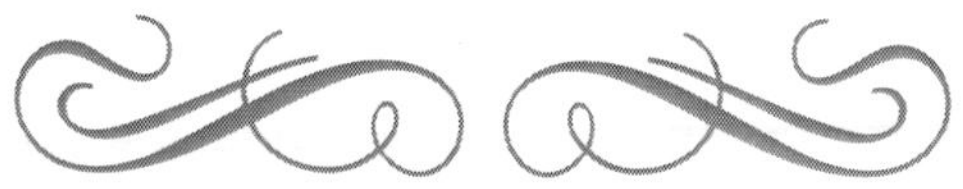

Down With...!

Winter 1927

Not until Ralph and I set foot on the waterfront at Foochow did we realize that something was in fact wrong. As we climbed the plank to the muddy embankment, we could see in both directions a solid mass of people. This time they weren't running or shoving, just standing still, staring silently. Hundreds, thousands. Even the entrances into the narrow streets and the overhanging balconies were filled. Another mob scene. Oh, damn! Oh, why? I looked longingly back at the river.

Rickshaw pullers approached reluctantly at our call, and we climbed in. As I was the lightest, the big yellow suitcase was put in with me. It stood upright between my feet, and as we jerked this way and that in the crowd, I had to balance it between my legs. This crowd? What did it mean?

At first my head was pounding too hard for me to see anything clearly. The rickshaw men instead of running had to walk, slowly, pushing people aside with the shafts. Then I began to look at faces—there were no friendly smiles, yet no threats. Everyone stared at us, their faces showing surprise, astonishment. "What are you foreigners doing here?" they asked. There was a pressure upon us from the thousands of eyes, but no motion of violence.

I glanced back and saw the other rickshaw close behind. The way that opened for us closed again quickly. Such a narrow street, hemming us in. Feeling trapped, I glanced up and was startled to see, hanging from a wire above our heads, a large picture poster. Then I stared. A great black and white cartoon displayed a grotesque "foreigner" with a long, pointed nose, holding a bayonet on which was spitted a Chinese baby. Drops of vermillion blood dripped from the wound. "Down with!" screamed the huge Chinese characters we had learned to recognize.

A little farther I saw another poster with a "foreign devil" tossing babies into a steaming black caldron. How ugly they had made him! I would be afraid of him too, if that was what he looked like to me. As others see us, I thought, over and over down the street…as others see us…and my eyes swam as I clutched the arms of the rickshaw.

The pavement was uneven. Jerk—jerk, bump—bump, lurch, hang on to the bag. For over an hour, we crawled through that crowd. We were as much a part of it as an electric switch is of its light. Push the switch and something will explode. When I looked back, Ralph smiled stiffly at me.

At last the city wall…through the city gate…into the old city. My puller hesitated as the crowd pressed in stopping us. No, I cried silently, no. A policeman stepped forward and pushed the people back, opening a way. Another policeman, and another. They were helping us through! So we made the long block to the entrance of Peace Street—our empty lane. And at last our compound gate…locked!

We pounded. "*Ioah, Ioah*, open the door!"

"Who is it?"

"It's Choi Sinang. Open please."

The gateman coughed. "I have orders not to open, for anyone. The soldiers will come in."

"No, no. There are no soldiers here."

Slowly the heavy iron bar was drawn back and the double gate opened a crack. Ioah peered through, then widened the crack so we could slide in.

In the compound we met Mr. Christian, white and shaken and strangely dressed in a cut-away. He stared. "Where did you come from?"

"The university."

"But didn't they warn you? The streets? The soldiers?"

"No. What has happened?"

"You don't *know* what has happened? The whole city is rioting against the foreigners. How could you ride through three miles of it and not know?"

"No one told us."

"Well, you're alive. A miracle."

As we walked up to our house, he said, "When they tore my coat off…"

"They? Who?"

"The soldiers. A bunch of soldiers broke in through the little barred-up gate in the wall behind Dr. Beard's house, waving bayonets. They looted his house and the Lewises'—everything they could get their hands on. When they started up the walk, I stopped them. They took my glasses—the chief's got them on now. And my one and only coat. They pulled a leg off my trousers so I had to run for cover. My others were all at the tailors. This is the first outfit I could find." He laughed.

"You look swell. Did they loot all the houses?" I asked, glancing up the hill at ours sitting as calmly as ever behind our palm trees. *Our* home.

"No. The city fathers sent their soldiers in with more bayonets, and they drove the first soldiers out. They're going to throw a guard around our compound tonight."

"That's nice," said Ralph. "How do we know the guard won't start looting too?"

"They won't." He grinned. "They're the right wing."

"Oh, I see," I said. *What a government that had right wings that guarded and left wings that looted. So it isn't over after all*, I thought sadly. *There* had *to be a revolution—if only it could be a friendly revolution! What next?*

We went into our house. Everything was as we had left it. Good home—it reached around us in its welcome.

As I was unpacking the yellow suitcase, Mary Campbell came up the walk and put the basket containing her five-month-old baby on the verandah.

"Hi there," she called. "Too bad you missed the fun."

"Come in, Mary. What are you doing here?"

"Came to see Neil, for a heart examination. Yes, no kidding. And worse luck, I brought my whole wardrobe of five dresses to see if Ing-ho would make them over. The confounded soldiers made off with the whole lot."

"You'll probably find them hanging in the thieves market someday. What happened?"

"I was on the bed in Alice's room having a heart examination. We heard smashing and yelling, and they burst in on us. One snatched my wrist and took my wrist watch and another grabbed the new Australian blankets I'd just received for Jane."

I glanced at Jane wrapped in a faded cotton blanket. She looked like a pink American doll in the Chinese bamboo basket with hood and carrying handles.

"Did they get much of Al's stuff?"

"Everything...but they didn't get our babies!"

It was a triumphal cry, strangely familiar as though I had heard it down the centuries.

She continued, "They're having a get-together down at the Christians' in a few minutes. Better come. May I sleep here tonight?"

"You bet. Alice had better come too." Our house, farthest from the gate, seemed safest. And it would be good to stay together. "You can leave Jane here."

"Not on your life. Where I go, Jane goes." And she walked down the hill carrying the basket with her.

I watched her numbly. Where would we be a day from now? A week from now? I was glad I did not have a child. The sun was setting and the White Pagoda reflected the cloud-flaming sky. So it had for a thousand years. Comforting permanence.

Gradually the compound families gathered in the small living room at the Christians'. Fear was disguised. They teased Mr. Christian about his cut-away. Alice hoped the soldiers would know how to work the percolator and would fully appreciate her snapshot album. Mary sat with Jane still sleeping in the fragile bamboo basket beside her.

Mr. Christian gave a review of events as gleaned from Chinese friends. Two British teachers had been driven through the streets to the cries of "Kill! Kill!" The British doctor was badly beaten and left for dead, but after the soldiers left, he had been picked up and hidden by friendly Chinese neighbors. The orders from someone had been, "Kill the British. Loot the Americans." Rumor said the left wing, angered by being thwarted, might put on a return engagement tonight. The city government hoped to protect us. But Boxer tales had been revived. "Foreigners to blame for all China's troubles. Foreigners using the eyes of babies to make medicine." In the meantime there was nothing we could do but pray. And the prayers arose, "Almighty God, give us strength..." confident that God was listening and ready to heed.

The baby lay sleeping in her basket in the middle of the circle—like a little princess, I thought, whom the fairies had surrounded to bestow upon her their special gifts. Will the wicked fairy break though and cast her evil prophecy, or will the charmed people protect her?

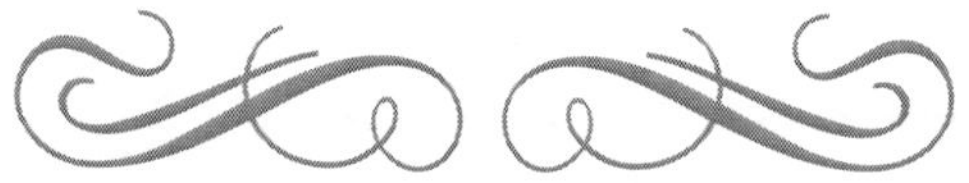

The Clock Strikes

Winter 1927

Alice refused to come to our house with her baby Grayanna. That night Mary and I dragged cots into the upstairs living room. Not that we would be any safer there in case of a raid but for the same reasons that ladies in days of old shut themselves in the innermost chambers of a castle. Shoes removed, we lay dressed, chilling in our cold beds. Jane slept in her basket, two cans of powdered milk and a bottle of boiled water at her feet. Through the cold night came the muffled voices of our husbands on guard in spite of the Chinese military whom we hadn't seen but who were supposedly out there in the night taking care of us.

At first, sleep was impossible. Then I imagined for myself a perfect pattern of life resuming its usual course in the morning. The sun would be shining, the teachers would come, we would go over to language class…

But in the morning it was not so easy to pick up the threads of life as I had supposed.

The teachers did not come.

What did we do about meals? Huo Seng suggested that it would be best for him not to go to the street to market.

What could we do? Study language by ourselves? Take a walk? The streets were filling with the same crowds as yesterday. We could see them from our hill. Should we pack? If so, what, and to go where? We were like people in a play who do not know their lines and have forgotten their cues.

People came and went, standing in little groups within the compound. Our seniors talked fluently in Chinese and then stopped talking if we came near. An elderly Chinese woman of large proportions and narrow faith came to each house and wept loudly. "If you go out there, they will kill you!"

At ten o'clock word was spread that at eleven the American consul would come, after a visit to the city officials, and give us instructions. I recalled the dictum—a British consul can order, but an American consul can only advise.

Outside our compound wall, we could see the crowds milling silently in the narrow street. At twelve o'clock we were still waiting. Huo Seng announced luncheon, but our men were nowhere to be found. Mary and I seated ourselves at distant points around the luncheon table, our pounding hearts choking us. Huo Seng pushed open the swing door and stood with dignity holding an enormous shepherd pie, his most crowning achievement. We gasped. Not one of us could imagine eating even a small portion of it. He served us with gentle insistence, saying silently: "Here is hot food. You need it. You must eat."

We did not dare hurt his feelings, but the food rolled around in our dry mouths. I looked at Mary. I could count her pulse beats in her throat.

This was too unreal—like Cinderella's ball gone wrong. If the clock were going to strike twelve, why did it not strike and be done with it?

When we were half through luncheon, Ralph and Mr. Christian appeared, bustling with decision.

"Women and children to South Side. The government is sending military escort to take you there. Leave in an hour. One suitcase per person. The men will stay to guard the property," Ralph explained.

"If you stay, I stay!"

"Oh, no you don't. These are orders."

"The consul can't order, he can only advise."

"We're going to follow his advice."

"Mrs. Beard won't go. You know she won't."

"Mrs. Beard is a law unto herself. Be reasonable. You know…in case we have to climb over the back wall. By the way, have you heard the news?"

"News? You don't say."

"About eighty people have already left from the South Side on the U.S.S. *Pillsbury*."

"Do they know where they're going?"

"Manila."

"Oh."

Fun. Packing a bag. For where? Manila? Shanghai? The South Seas? America?

For how long? For what emergencies?

At least there was no doubt about one thing. Heavy underwear for the raw weather in this unheated world. Underwear, wool stockings, and sweaters filled most of our suitcases.

There was little space left. I looked around. I walked through the rooms. Then I realized that the clock had struck, without my hearing it. So this was the end. The sun shone in the living room window on the new wicker table where our choicest American books stood between carved bookends. Never before had home looked so terribly lovely. What bit of this beauty could I salvage? Quickly I snatched a Nanking tapestry from under the books, then climbed on a chair and untacked the Japanese batik from over the dining room fireplace. I folded them into a small square and stuffed them into one end of the suitcase.

At the gatehouse our women and children were gathering. We waited. Outside down below we could see the crowds in the streets. What have I left that's important? I know I've left something necessary. What is it? What could it be? Oh, I know. May I run back to the house? No. Oh, please. The guard will be here any minute.

The weeping woman had come to cheer us on. "Don't go out in those streets. They'll kill you." Somebody tactfully removed her. We gave our husbands last-minute advice. "There are canned goods in the cupboard. The key is—let me see. Here it is, around my neck."

The four Leger children were enjoying the excitement—a pleasant break in their home routine of studies.

Agnes pointed across the gatehouse roof into the street below. "Look, the carriages are coming."

Someone answered, "There they are. Oh, only three carriages. We can't all go in three."

Someone else said, "Where's the guard?"

Like Cinderella coaches after the clock had struck, the three small carriages drew up outside the gate, bells clanging, small urchins dragging at the unwilling little ponies—dusty and moth-eaten.

Bobby Leger caught his mother's hand. "Mother, did you know our little almond tree is just beginning to blossom?"

"Oh, Bobby, why…"

"Come on," shouted the men. "Here comes the fourth carriage. You can all go."

We ran down the steps, out the gate, the gate that kept us safe, and piled into the tiny carriages. Alice and Grayanna got into the third carriage with me. We had barely room for our knees and the bags. The floor of the carriage looked uncertain. Sometimes the floor fell out and the tires came off. The pony was very wobbly.

"Good-bye, you'll be coming back in a couple of days."

"Don't forget to feed the cat," Alice called.

The bells clanged. The footman pulled at the pony's bridle. We were off.

Strange how a street that has been your friend may suddenly change—become an altogether different place, a living enemy. The very color, size, contour seems different. Where was the brass shop where we had bargained with the friendly master for a piece of shining brass? Not there. Not anywhere behind those rows of staring eyes.

Now the city wall and gate. The ponies' hoofs clattered under the vaulted dome. This was the third time in four days. When would be the next? Would there be a next?

The "foreign devil" banners were still across the road, but we could not see them well from within the closed coaches. Near the Bridge of Ten Thousand Ages on the edge of a clearing we saw dead bodies. We pretended not to see them. Our pony, moving at a snail's pace, was visibly weakening. Sometimes the head carriage stopped. Then we stopped too, unable to see the cause. Forward and stop. Forward and stop. *Flight for life,* I thought. *How like China.*

In the middle of the narrow Bridge of Ten Thousand Ages, our small pony succumbed. He went down on his shaky knees. The driver whipped, but no amount of brutal beating encouraged him to get up. The footman swore and tugged at his bridle. We saw the first two carriages going heartlessly on and the swift Min River rushing beneath.

A crowd gathered around. They saw our plight, laughed and shook their heads with sympathy. An argument ensued.

"The horse can't walk," said one, pointing at the fallen creature.

"Yes, he can," shouted the irate carriage driver.

"No, can't you see? He has no strength."

"He has strength. He is simply stubborn."

"No. You can count his ribs. You have not given him enough to eat. He is a poor, miserable sore-eyed starved beast, and he has no strength to pull such a great load."

"You lie," shouted the driver, lashing his whip. "He is a great, strong horse, but he has a devil in him."

Laughing, the onlookers got on either side and with a pull, raised the great horse to his trembling feet.

"Now you shall see," called the driver. And with jouncing motion, we resumed the flight for our lives.

"Why, they're a friendly mob," said Alice, breathing again.

"It's the soldiers that don't like us," I said.

At last we could see the winding roads leading up the hill to the South Side Community. Safety...at least, of a sort.

We were billeted in a mid-Victorian house, dark with emptiness. The servants were closing the shutters of all the deserted houses—like the eyes of dead people. Most of the women and children of South Side had left on the U.S. destroyer that morning. Here Gertrude joined us.

Some man-in-charge told us to come to an important meeting at the consulate, a short walk away. We saw the American flag waving bravely at the top of its tall pole—the Stars and Stripes Forever. You're American citizens... nothing can hurt you here, it waved. We who had so boldly disclaimed "gunboat diplomacy" found our eyes moist.

It was a serious meeting—men with grave faces consulting, questioning. A second gunboat was on the way. There were rumors, through Chinese friends, that an attack was planned on this island of foreign business houses and the Methodist mission, its schools, and hospital. Finally they gave us explicit instructions—a plan for your safety. If they come over by the Big Bridge, you will flee down the lane behind the bank (where was the bank?) to the public jetty. If they cross at Upper Bridge, take the road past Nang Sang's to the customs landing.

Please, how would we know?

The consulate would fire a gun…three shots if they come by Big Bridge, five if by Upper Bridge. To be repeated at intervals.

Gertrude leaned toward me. "One if by land, two if by sea," she said with mock solemnity. In spite of the grave situation, we giggled.

But we slept again with our clothes on. That night was very black. Usually, even in extremities, one has a vague idea of what the next day holds in store. One can see, however dimly, into it. But that night for us the future was cut off. A black curtain had dropped in heavy folds before us—too heavy to push aside—impenetrable.

The attack did not come. The next morning was bright, but to the three of us wives without our husbands, cold and forbidding. Gertrude and I dressed, shivering, in the large old bedroom.

The following day, after the South Side families had left for Manila, Hong Kong, or America, the consul turned his attention to us from the city.

"You can go to Pagoda Anchorage. Hire a private launch and go down on the tide tomorrow at eleven."

E-Song arrived with our silver and cheerful messages from the men. "Still alive. Hope you are the same." We sent back frantic appeals for more clothes. "Get them to the jetty before eleven."

The time arrived…five minutes before eleven. We were inside the cabin of the small launch, and no E-Song. Suddenly we saw a sampan pull alongside. Ah, here was Nieng-Nu, the mason, with two large baskets. And *Ralph*! Through the cabin window, we saw the sampan rolling and bobbing on the fast tide of the rushing water. The sampan men shouted as they lowered the baskets through the launch cabin door.

"Aren't you coming with us?" I called to Ralph. "Come, please come."

"No, I can't. Neil and Arthur send their love. Have fun!"

The launch engine vibrated. The sampan bobbed up and down. We started threading our way among the painted hulls of the seagoing junks. Leaning from the launch window, I saw the sampan heading laboriously back, disappearing behind a junk with a staring black and white eye, and Ralph's white sun helmet disappearing with it.

Halfway between Foochow and the sea, at Pagoda Anchorage, the Min River spread to a broad basin where we had disembarked three and a half months before. On a hill overlooking the busy river, one of our doctors had built, years ago, a spacious white home and a compact hospital. He took care of the sick for miles around and had been given the commission of Port Doctor. Whenever a ship raised its yellow flag, he chugged out to it on his sampan with an outboard to see that cholera and plague not spread into the land. The old doctor and his family had gone home on furlough. Mary and Horace Campbell were taking their places for the year. "Won't Horace and Mary be surprised?" we said.

We had dinner at the white house on the hill, which had the only extension table in Foochow. Dinner that night was an occasion—lighted candles. Horace at one end, Mary at the other. Eleven of us, women and children, in between. Jane and Grayanna asleep on the porch.

The cook's two sons served.

"Isn't this jolly," said Horace. peering around the lighted candles at each of us. "Father, Mother, and all the children. But what I want to know is why you all came *here*?"

"Don't ask us. Ask the consul," said Mrs. Leger.

"But the consul can't order, he can only advise."

"I tell you, he's playing chess, and I think he's winning," said Gertrude.

Alice was stubborn. "He's not going to win over me. I'm going back the first possible chance."

"Cheerio, Alice, that's the spirit." Horace beamed approval.

"Horace, how can you talk that way?" said Mary, looking around the candles at him.

Alice persisted, "I don't believe in separations. Didn't we say 'For better, for worse'?"

"What about your baby?" gently asked Mrs. Leger. She looked along the table at her three girls and boy, quite accustomed now to putting their needs first.

"Of course I'm thinking of Grayanna. She needs her father. And she can't sleep without her crib."

Horace shouted, "Good, Alice. That's the spirit."

Bobby Leger wiggled excitedly. "Mother...Mother! Will we ever get to eat those beets we planted in our garden?"

"Our wedding presents, we hadn't unpacked them yet." Gertrude moaned. "Now how can we write the thank you notes?"

"Our wedding pictures...a lot of crazy ones in that album the looters carried off."

"Mother, we can't study. We haven't our books." Agnes Leger was elated.

Mary looked around disgustedly. "You people make me sick talking about *things*. They could have my five dresses and everything else I own when they didn't get our babies!"

"Or our husbands, don't forget," added Gertrude. We laughed. Arthur, the Viking—imagine anyone running off with him!

"Good girls," said Horace.

"Do you think it will be in the American papers?" asked Gertrude. "I think we're being caught in a page of history."

Suddenly we sobered, feeling small and helpless, knowing we were caught in something so much larger than our own little private destinies. I looked around at the candle-lit faces, shadowed from the suspense of the last days…were we experiencing the end of an era? Change was the wind blowing from the nostrils of the awakening Chinese dragon. White Man was being blown from his high mountain. I wondered if the others were all praying, as I was: Let this wind blow for the good of both our lands.

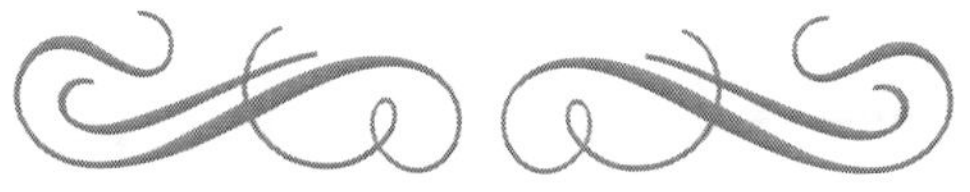

Quivering Web

Winter 1927

Life in the white house at Pagoda Anchorage settled into a pattern without meaning. The past seemed purposeless, and the future, a catastrophe, perhaps, held in abeyance. I thought if I could get up high enough and look down, I could see what was going to happen. But there was no way to get up. We were caught like flies in a quivering web, and the days were filled with endless waiting. For what?

And how long can suspense last? In time one becomes numb to it, so that instead of constant dread of something-that-may-happen, one almost hopes for something-to-happen to put an end to the tension that has become unendurable.

Day after day was like this. Day after day we did not know what we might hear from the city about our husbands, our homes, even what might be about to happen to ourselves.

Physically life settled into a simple routine. Making use of cots and settees, we fourteen women and children slept in the two bedrooms and porch. Duai-die, the cook, was literally Lord-of-the-Kitchen. More people, more food. More food, more squeeze. He was content but crusty, and we kept out of his way.

No language teacher would come to us. We tried to write letters, but that was difficult. The raw winter settled into the house, turning it into an oversized refrigerator. Outside there was at least freshness, with the wet wind sweeping in from the sea, but inside, it settled into a dank chill that penetrated everyone's bones and tempers. Coal was too expensive and scarce, except for a small grate fire in the evenings. Putting on extra clothes didn't help, seeming to shut in the cold and making it difficult to move. Our fingers soon grew too stiff to function with pen or typewriter. When we read we wrapped steamer rugs around us and pulled on gloves, but even so the cold was stronger than the book. Anyway, what should we write? We didn't know what was happening in China. "We are fine. We have nothing to do but wait. It is cold—the temperature almost down to freezing. We all have chilblains on our fingers and toes. They itch terribly." How would that sound in America where it was near zero? They couldn't understand the cold—the dead cold of an unheated house. Or this waiting. I closed my eyes and could hear the sizzling of the steam heat in the home we had left in America. At meal times we went to the long table wrapped in steamer rugs, and when it was coldest, from each person we could see puffs of breath. Duai-die did his best to serve hot food, but there was little he had to work with—tough, stringy pork from the razorback pigs, sweet potatoes, bean sprouts or greens of mustard leaves. Rice. Day after day. We began to dream of juicy steaks, apple pie, cheese, cow's milk and cream and butter, instead of this queer white stuff from the water buffalo cows.

Each day we watched the kitchen door hoping for a change. Faces grew bleak, except for Gertrude. Closing her eyes, as Hua-hiong, the cook's son approached, she would murmur, "Ah, juicy rare T-bones. Thought I smelled them cooking."

"Can it, for the love of Pete!" Horace would shout, picking up his water glass.

Gertrude would look amazed. "Why, I thought it was."

Gertrude, Alice, and I tried to keep warm by walking. Sometimes we followed the stone walk connecting villages along the Min River. It led us through narrow, crooked streets over slimy cobblestones around the razorback sows with the unbelievable litters.

The villagers would nod, friendly puzzled nods to us, then pointing, and say in Chinese to a neighbor, "Which is it, a man or a woman?"

"A woman, of course. Can't you tell?"

But one afternoon in a far village there was real bewilderment. Men or women? Nudges and whispers. "Why men, they must be. See their short hair. And look, what big feet!"

One day we heard a commotion as we turned into a narrow lane in the village at the foot of our hill. There, in front of a fruit stall, stood a group of sailors from an American gunboat that had anchored in the harbor a few days before. There they stood against the gray of the street, in their whites and white caps, stuffing tangerines into their pockets. Suddenly they bolted not paying the copper coins they owed. They ran quickly down the rough cobbles, the orange fruit flashing in their hands, turned a corner and were gone. The shopkeepers stood aghast then sent curses flying after them. A wrinkled old woman with trembling hands re-piled the tumbled fruit in her stall, shaking her head and counting her loss. We turned back, not wishing to be seen.

Sometimes we hiked over the hills above the house, scrambling over unused paths and lumpy grave mounds while the wind whipped the brown weedy grass flat around the old stone markers. Around the house someone had planted gracious tropical trees, but the hills were bare except for ugly yucca plants with their scratchy spikes.

We discovered on this brow of a hill the remains of an old fort. The cannon, falling apart with rust, still pointed outward commanding the entrance to the harbor. Underneath were crumbling half-buried passages. Beyond the fort the path came to a long low stone monument—a white slab marking a trench grave of two hundred Chinese sailors who had lost their lives defending the harbor from the French. A forgotten memorial of China's fruitless struggle to keep the West out.

The path led us on to the stone courtyard of a simple French Catholic orphanage. The sisters in long, full, black gowns and stiff white bonnets welcomed us from the cold wind. Proudly they took us through the convent. In a bare room upstairs, we watched Chinese orphans learning a trade, making fleur-de-lis in Pointe Venice lace. In the little chapel below with a candle burning before a crucifix, we watched the Chinese children worshiping a French God.

The embroideries from Sister Hilaire's Orphanage were known for the perfection of their design.

"*Mais li, encore.* We are lonely," she said, mixing her French and Chinese.

Later we were told that the orphanage had been closed. The nuns had been forced to flee for their lives. They had been taken to the river and put on a boat for the South. What had happened to the orphans? We never knew.

Horace warned us not to venture beyond the orphanage, though a red brick Chinese temple on the pine slope high above looked inviting. Not long before, he told us two Chinese had been brought to the hospital clawed by a leopard. One man died, and the other spent a long time recuperating. Later the family brought the doctor some leopard meat, to give him strength, they explained. It was very tough, Horace told us.

One day we were given an escort. The Chinese navy, consisting of one old Chinese-manned foreign ship, its headquarters in the harbor below, had offered to protect us. We weren't sure from what—leopards or revolution. Three barefooted lads with ragged uniforms and large antique guns appeared daily and sat on a low stone wall below our house. Endlessly they polished the guns, which always looked rusty. When we appeared in hiking clothes, they sighed, shouldered their guns, and followed us at a short distance. Wherever we went, scrambling up through yucca plants or exploring the old fort, they dragged obviously unwilling feet. Their guns flopped about in any and all directions. We felt as wary of those guns as of leopards.

Later an official messenger arrived. His note crisply requested that we remain within the boundaries of our own grounds. For how could the navy protect the lives of the foreigners if they persisted in climbing all over the mountains?

Dread, of what we did not know, always hung in the air. One black night when we were sleeping, frantic shouts, clash of brass cymbals, and the blare of horns crashed into my dreams. They were after me at last. I sat up in bed and tried to run. In the next beds Alice and Gertrude were sitting up—both listening.

Soldiers, I thought.

"Just a wedding," said Alice.

"No, a funeral," Gertrude said.

"An idol procession," I suggested.

The awful noise came closer reaching the bluff above our house, and we stopped breathing. With a great blast of sound, it moved off down the hill.

Gertrude said, "Halloween!" We chuckled, lay down and pretended to go to sleep. At least it was not the revolution!

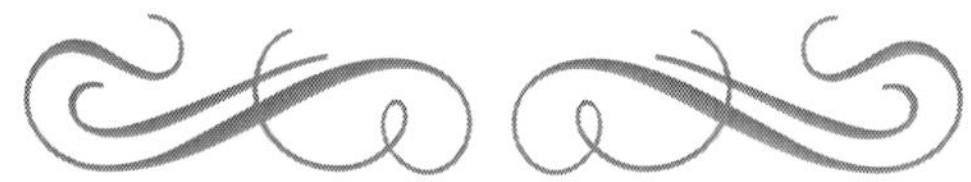

The Shattered Wall

February 1927

Suddenly the suspension cord was cut—we were let down to earth with a bang. The consul sent a telegram. Everybody was to be evacuated. That is, everybody who wasn't important. A few necessary people could stay, but no more than could be removed at a moment's notice in case of emergency.

Rumor reported another division of antiforeign army approaching Foochow. Questions of foreign policies were at stake. Questions that had to do with extraterritoriality, unequal treaties, tariff control. Daily threats of attacks continued. White people were tools of imperialism. Better to clear out than to be the cause of an "incident" of international complications.

Boats were sailing for Shanghai, Hong Kong, Formosa (modern name Taiwan). Take your choice. Shanghai was already overflowing with refugees. Hong Kong also. Might it not all blow over? There was Formosa nearby. Camphor and spicy tea, we had heard, and head hunters stealing through jungle paths with curved knives gleaming at their belts.

The message reached all the scattered members of our mission—those in the city, up river, the country, and down river. We would imagine the consternation. Close our hospital? Close our schools? What about the patients? The students? Special runners were sent from one to another. What are you going to do? Does this mean me? Unthinkable, just now…

So a big council meeting was to be held. They were all, including Ralph, Neil, and Arthur, coming down the river to Pagoda Anchorage to have it with us in peace and safety. We brought all the chairs in the house to the living room and built a big fire in the fireplace to welcome them. A fire—ahhh!

It was a terribly important meeting. They sat facing the fire but not seeing it. Just thinking…thinking and feeling. And then they started talking. The eyes of some were bitter, seeing the past as it had been and seeing the future as they feared it would be, a crushed, broken thing.

What was to happen? Give over all the work to the Chinese?

For eighty years, these white people had been coming across the seas and building their lives in with the lives of the people of China. Here in the blind, ruthless impact of West on East was a small flame of friendship, of understanding, a glowing thing. Each man saw in it his own loved piece of work. His university, his hospital, his agricultural school. Each was there to defend with his soul's blood the work of his life.

The group was divided into two camps. The older generation, who saw the work of eighty years crashing to ruin around them. The younger generation, though this was not a matter of age, who now saw a chance for the past eighty years to bear fruit.

The dean presided, wisely, objectively, but with a gentleness as though wishing to soften the suffering of those who must suffer. With short, almost silent words, he recognized one after another as they stood.

A man who had spent the best part of his life in the business aspects of the mission rose to speak of deeds, properties long struggled for and developed, trust funds. Turn everything over? Impossible!

A wrinkled, energetic woman who had lived a span of seventy years in the land and knew the city from the highest Mandarin home to the filthiest jail interrupted to back him up. "I know the Chinese. There is not one who wants the financial responsibility. His whole clan would be upon his neck."

Another said with irony, "I suppose you have stopped to consider this would mean that the calling back of Americans after furloughs and the allocating of us to our work would be in the hands of the Chinese."

Someone answered, "It is their land. In whose hands could it better be?"

Some of the women brought their knitting, but their needles stopped flashing and a yarn ball rolled unheeded to the floor.

"If there is nothing to return to…" said the man of titles and deeds. He closed his eyes wearily as if he had suddenly grown old.

It became a struggle. First one side, then the other… on and on. A struggle of wills. Of souls. Trying to find a harmonic solution to a symphony that threatens to break down after a climax of crashing discord.

Assurance…fear. Faith…doubt.

"We must turn over our high positions to our Chinese. Don't forget their great culture, their ability… it is their turn."

"We cannot do it. The Chinese are not yet established in the ways of Western institutions and business management."

"For eighty years they have been learning."

"Still they are not ready. There are too few with experience in these things."

"They will learn by experience."

"While they learn the institutions we have built will crash about their ears."

"Suppose they do. If the gold of truth is here in what we have brought them, it will remain. Truth is not dependent on institutions."

"But we cannot do this thing—build up these institutions and, the minute we are in danger, run for our lives?"

"The problem is not a matter of danger to us. Every white man these days is the symbol of imperialism. We must remove that symbol."

(Ah, there was the path we all could take!)

"We, who claim to be friends, must give up the last vestige of imperialism, shift the leadership to them. But we must stand by and help them adjust the load to their shoulders."

"And you think they are ready?"

"It is our mistake if we have not made them ready. *Mei-yu fa-tze.* There is no other way."

"Then let us pray about it."

And they prayed, first silently, then in turn, while the fire threw its light and shadow over bowed heads and pale, tense faces. Some trying to make God see their way. Others trying truly to see God's way.

They put the question to a vote. One man left the room, his lips compressed and white, unable to witness the moment that would bring his life's work tumbling to the ground.

Oh, God, give the Chinese a chance. They can do it. We know they can.

We young ones were not allowed to vote. But how we hoped. How we thought we understood these young Chinese suffering so proudly under foreign superiorism. Our eyes met quietly across the circle.

Give them the positions they ought to have. If we don't, there's no use in our staying. We might just as well go back to America.

We looked at each other. Hope—fear—held in check. If only…

The question was stated, clearly, irrevocable, like the pronouncement of a sentence. And then they rose to be counted, slowly, a few at a time till all but two were standing. All but one. Then yes, even he of the deeds and titles. All were on their feet to vote, "that we may relinquish all positions of authority and turn those positions over to our Chinese coworkers."

Yes, Micah, and walk humbly before thy God.

Before the day was over messages were sent to five young Chinese, some with degrees not yet completed, some across the seas in America, or England, asking them to return and be principals and presidents of the institutions and the executive head of the mission.

A leap forward. Was it in the dark? Who could tell?

And three days later those of us who weren't important left for Formosa.

The Seikyo Maru moved down the mouth of the Min River past the pointed little islands at Sharp Peak. Nodding to them, I said to Ralph, "Four and a half months since we saw those islands. Four and a half months in China—and we've done nothing…just exactly nothing." I thought of the Chinese students across our wall.

He touched my hand. "Wait a minute. Maybe we haven't. Maybe we're helping most by leaving now…for a time. But we've *seen*, haven't we? And we've learned. We've learned that there *had* to be a revolution!"

"Do you think we'll have another chance? Oh, I hope it's not too late. I hope there'll be another chance."

Then the sea grew very rough. I thought, *That Chinese dragon again!*

Part II

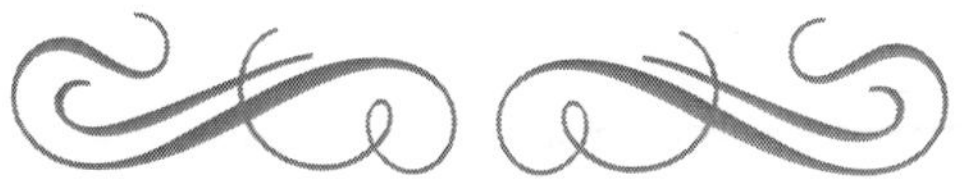

Return

June 1927

It was early June 1927, in the bare Formosa house where we had found temporary shelter.

"Listen," Ralph exclaimed. "Listen to this!" and placed the second set of headphones on my ears.

The Shanghai radio broadcast came in blurred—the batteries weak now, and the static strong. But the message came through, authorized, they said, by Chiang Kai-shek himself:

> Inform all foreigners who have left China during the troubles of the past months—we invite you to return—open your schools, hospitals, and businesses. The Nationalist Kuomintang Government will do everything in its power to protect you.

Transferring the headphones to Gertrude and Arthur, they heard the repeat with excited nods.

Yes...we could go back to China! After four and a half months of impatient waiting in the misty rains of Formosa, at last we could go back to our China home. We could pick up the threads of our revolution-interrupted lives!

On the night of June 22, on an even smaller boat than the one on which we had arrived, we retraced our way across that dragon-tossed channel.

After a stormy night, we climbed limply on deck and saw, so close, the rock-crested range of the Fukien Mountains. Passing the jagged island, Sharp Peak, we moved into the mouth of the sparkling Min River. What would we find? Would this return to China be a reprieve—a chance to fulfill our dreams?

I asked, "Do you think our home is damaged? Will our friends who left return?"

Ralph answered with his own question, asking "Will Huo-seng and E-song return to us? How could we eat, drink, and be clean without them? Or has the propaganda frightened them hopelessly away?"

Gertrude and Arthur were concerned about where their baby would be born. They did not have a house yet. I suggested: "You could join us at our rented house on the mountain this summer, and when the baby arrives, Ralph and I could go elsewhere for a few days."

But I was concerned whether there would be a doctor on the mountain. I did not want to be a midwife as I had feared I might have to be all last night on that rough sea.

Arthur wondered if he would be able to get to the country where he wanted to work. Or would there be too many bandits around? Gertrude shuddered.

Gertrude and I hoped the Nationalist Army had stopped pasting so much antiforeign propaganda on the walls. Had they, or *somebody*, got the soldiers under control? Would we be able to start now to live normally—to have the homes we had hoped for, where our children (when we had them) could live in reasonable security? Not too much, of course—this was China! But enough so we wouldn't have to flee through mobs again, and be separated from our husbands while they "protected the property" in a city threatened by attack.

No matter—we were going home—Foochow where we lived, where we could speak a few mispronounced words of the language, where we had work to do.

At last—the familiar wide harbor, river junks with patched brown sails, Pagoda Anchorage—familiar shouting from the sampan women, familiar sound of the anchor chain clanging down. We crowded at the rail. Ah, there was the launch from the city to meet us. And *look*! Huo-seng, in his second-best long-coat, looking like a teacher with his silver gray hair, nodding and smiling at us. Excitedly we waved. There was Mr. Leger who had remained in Foochow through all the trouble. It was a family reunion.

The launch ride up the river, the rickshaws, honking through the crowded streets—it was all as if we had never been away. At the compound gate E-song, smiling broadly, helped us in with our many bundles.

And when that evening we had eaten a good dinner and our mosquito nets were hung, how comforting to go to sleep in our own beds! Our house had not been harmed, and we slept in its welcome like children.

The next day, however, we immediately repacked into twenty loads of bamboo baskets to go to Kuliang, our mountain summer resort. Two months of escape from the Season of Great Heat, as the Chinese called it, and its handmaiden, cholera. Two months of language study, punctuated with tennis and mountain hikes, and the arrival of Gertrude's baby.

When we returned from the mountain in September, we found the city bustling with eager life, the New Day, girls with short bobbed hair and shorter skirts, *and* propaganda. Walls were covered with fresh posters: "Up with Equal Rights for Women!...Up with the Eight-Hour Day!..." and the familiar "Down with..." slogans, to which a new one was added, "Down with the Communists!"

So...Chiang Kai-shek had split with the Communists!

After his successful march north that spring of 1927, convinced that cooperation with the capitalist nations was essential for his party's aims of building a strong and sometime democratic nation, he established his capital at Nanking(modern name Nanjing), and sent his Russian advisors home. His government also launched a purge of Chinese communists, especially in south China where they were the strongest.

Most of China's students were involved in this struggle, feeling as they had for more than a generation that there had to be a revolution. As literates they became spokesmen and agitators for China's illiterate masses. In our own college no one knew which students, or even faculty members, were Communist sympathizers. We only hoped we would not hear the fire gongs booming again at night.

The days were troubled too.

We were advised not go to out on the streets. When we did, and saw soldiers coming, we slid into the nearest shop, and the friendly shopkeepers appeared to take no notice of us.

Our servants also had their problems. Soldiers would sometimes grab a sturdy man—*nieh*—they called it, and press him into service carrying loads, pricking his rear with a bayonet.

Sometimes, with sick hearts, we saw groups of unhappy men roped together, being pushed through the streets by gruff captors. To what end? We never knew. It was a relief to get back within the walls of our compound.

If, on our return to Foochow, we had expected that the revolution was over and China had it made, we had much to learn—so much! Take for example, the battle. We never had believed that a battle could take place over our heads!

To understand how this could happen in a city trying to leap into the "modern" day would be to understand the rule by warlords, which had been a long shadow in Chinese history.

Though there was a central government, through the centuries, with tenuous fingers that reached out through its vast empire—that built canals and levied taxes, and though there were civil magistrates, the power was in the hands of the ones who had weapons. Bandit chief or warlord, depending on who was top man—their soldier-bandits swarmed the countryside.

Through the years the city people thought, *Let us look well to our strong walls and iron-barred gates.* They did this and built apertures above the gates through which to pour vats of boiling water. They hired mercenaries to do the pouring.

Our city had such walls and gates and its own "military" of sorts. Foochow desired above everything to have a strong "military" that did not prey on the people and could protect the city from the famous up-country *Tupi*, Lu Ting-bang, whose name made the country villagers stare in terror.

This man controlled large sections of Fukien Province and had long had his eye on Foochow, the provincial capital. Here, near the mouth of the river, the business of the province flowed, and taxes could be most profitable. His many underlings staked out the river country for their own individual claims.

Our friends who traveled upriver had often to ride in armor-protected river-boats and dodge the bullets of the *Tupi* along the shore, as well as pay stiff "likin" charges to buy protection through each group's territory. Several had been captured, to return with stories of the pathetic lot of these roving bandits—men neither good nor bad, but hungry, and knowing no other way to live in the impoverished land.

Other friends wrote of the burning of small villages, the times when farmers, begging protection, hurried to the foreign school compounds or churches. It was the normal way of life, building up to pitches of excitement when Lu Ting-bang himself approached the city gates with his poorly clad followers and their antiquated but noisy guns.

So always our big city must be constantly on guard and able to defend itself with its own "military."

Now the Nationalist Government, eager to stop this factional nonsense and "unify China," sometimes added another element of surprise to this normal chaos.

But we in the city behind the thick stone walls felt smugly secure from such surprises—until the day of the battle.

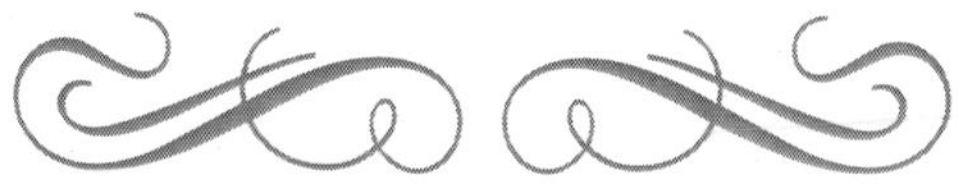

The Battle

Fall 1927

We had no warning that anything was wrong, that bright morning of October thirteenth in the fall of 1927. The day before we had watched a welcome parade for some visiting general, with festive banners and firecrackers. Everyone seemed happy.

And there were those necessary errands. So Agnes and I, weighing the chronic unrest against the lure of the sunny day, decided to go shopping on South Street.

Outside the compound gate, we noticed at once the emptiness of the street—not a single rickshaw waited. We walked hesitantly along the narrow way between walls, past the noodle-maker's shop, the Confucian temple, the entrance to the small yamen (a military headquarters)—a five-minute walk to South Street. Still no rickshaws. *Very* strange. But the shops were open, so we continued to the big cloth stores with their bolts of gay Japanese cotton cloth and Chinese silks, and usually eager shopkeepers.

Today the clerks gave us little attention. I did not like the way they stood with small groups in front of the shops, talking, talking, talking…

I didn't like it when, as we were in the back of a shop, everyone rushed to the front, and looked out into the street at the sound of shouting. Before we could see the cause of the disturbance, it had gone by.

At a shop farther on we heard shouting again. Agnes was at the door, and as I started toward her, she said, "Don't look. Don't look."

So of course I looked. And there was a crowd of soldiers hauling along a stumbling fellow who'd had the back of his head bashed in and fresh blood streaming down his blue coat.

I said, "Let's get home."

As we retraced our steps, we noticed the streets were now strangely quiet. Everywhere people stood in little groups…talking. We hurried past the jade shops, where we had planned to stop with Christmas in mind, and got into the compound as the noon gun boomed. I heard Agnes sigh as the old gatekeeper barred the gate behind us.

At luncheon we reported to Ralph, and Horace and Mary who were living with us temporarily. We talked on, oblivious to a distant percussion of firecrackers, which played a frequent theme through the noise of a Chinese city. Some change in the sound suddenly made us sit up and listen.

"Firecrackers," Ralph commented serenely after a minute and continued to eat.

"Funny sounding firecrackers," said Horace, who did not continue eating. "Sounds like firecrackers under a dishpan."

"Or a wooden tub," said Ralph, listening again.

"Guns?" Mary and I said at once. "Must be guns! Rifles!"

"How would you girls know?" asked Horace and walked to the dining room window, which from the top of our hill gave us a view over the city to the north.

Goose pimples ran up my back. No…no…please not guns! It couldn't be…here in the city. Ralph was at the window that looked out over the compound wall.

"It must be!" he exclaimed.

"Nice of them to wait till we got home," said Agnes, who always rose with spirit to any emergency.

E-Song pushed open the swinging door from the kitchen, waving his usually quiet arms. "*Pung*! *Pung-aah*! They shoot…shoot guns! Come see!"

We all ran out to the long tile balustrade back of our house. Looking over the wall below us, over the curved roofs of Chinese houses, we could see the upper part of the large yamen, headquarters of some faction of the military. The street was hidden from view but from it drifted up trails of smoke, and the sharp crack of rifles came faster, and closer. Guns—unmistakably!

Now Huo-seng joined us.

"What's it all about?" Ralph asked him.

Pale, but maintaining his dignity, he shrugged. "*Bing-ding*…*tupi*—soldiers…bandits…who knows?"

Others joined us—the Legers from the house below, and the servants from Dr. Dyer's house adjoining ours. Then came the servants from the houses lower on our hill. One of these, running toward us pointed back to the hillside above us below the Chinese temple.

"Look! Look! Big guns…it's a real battle!"

As we ran to the front of our house to look where he pointed, it came—the fast, loud stuttering of a machine-gun firing. This I heard before only in imagination. Now the sound bounced in reality from the brick walls all about our heads. I was numb with disbelief.

On the hillside, too close, we could see soldiers kneeling behind boulders, frantically loading and firing. We watched fascinated—seeing every motion of their arms—almost the whites of their eyes, Horace said. They were firing toward the big *yamen*, the shells bypassing us by a narrow margin.

Mary, standing by me, took one look, and crying "Jane!" dashed into the house. Jane, asleep in her crib on the porch next to the hillside, had not been disturbed. Quickly we pulled her bed into the inner room and returned to the balcony in the rear. We could not see down into the court of the *yamen*, but the firing continued in both directions. And now we could hear it also from across the compound, from Peace Street which skirted our hill past the White Pagoda, and the men's and women's hospitals. We were surrounded by this strange battle!

The Chinese on the balustrade seemed as puzzled as we were, and in doubt whether to take it seriously or not. This battle, apparently, was not aimed against the foreigners. It must be a personal skirmish, like those we had seen in the Chinese theatre. It did have a touch of the theatre—to us standing idly in the middle of it, hearing and smelling it, but not involved—at least not yet.

A Chinese tailor watching with us turned and ran into Dr. Dyer's house. The others called after him, "Why run away? No danger!"

He returned with his bright oiled paper umbrella, which he opened and held over his head. The others pointed laughing.

"What do you think, you numskull? The paper will stop a bullet?"

How they teased him! He laughed but continued to hold the umbrella over his head. However, when some bullets suddenly zinged against the tile roof of our house making chips fly, and others came whining close, we all ran back into the houses.

In our dining room, E-Song insisted on passing the rice pudding, which we tried to swallow to please him. But when a bullet cracked loudly against brick, we all stood, and Huo-seng, sticking a white face through the swing door, said, "Better get below!"

Horace said, "Bye, girls," and we saw him, ducking, run down the walk in the direction of the hospital.

Mary picked up Jane and her traveling basket. I went by the kitchen and gathered her warming luncheon, and then, heads crouching behind our protective garden wall, we ran down the outside back steps to our coal cellar.

We put the basket on the floor among the tall baskets of charcoal, and Jane, rosy and bright-eyed, stood holding the side of the basket, and jumped up and down laughing. The machine guns chattered.

Mary said, "It's a new tune to be stirring meat broth and Farina too!"

My mouth was dry, and my heart pounded as cracks of rifles answered machine guns—angry pelting antiphonal sounds above our heads. There for three hours we sat on hard benches, while the servants gathered in their cooking quarters, talking, talking…

In the beginning we hadn't realized the seriousness of what we thought merely a skirmish. It turned out to be a slaughter. Late in the afternoon the shots ceased, and Ralph and I went cautiously to reconnoiter. We went along the narrow street that skirted our wall toward the big yamen.

"Look out," said Ralph, and we flattened ourselves against the wall as barefoot soldiers with crude red-cross bands on their arms passed us carrying litters of wounded, groaning men with raw flesh and protruding bone and dripping blood. Near the yamen the dead were piled—more than thirty bodies, butchered by machine gun shells at the distance of a few yards. The sight lost all reality before my dizzying sickened eyes. I thought this is not possible—I am in a moving picture!

Quickly we turned and hurried back. We passed the men with the litters and read the question in their eyes. "To the hospital," we said, pointing, and they nodded.

We went to the hospital, and there, before long, we counted more than ninety pallets side by side on the floor down the entire length of the wide corridor. This in our bare, almost empty hospital—closed except for a large day clinic because of construction of a Union Hospital on the South Side of the city.

There lay almost a hundred men desperately needing help. The Chinese cry "*Ai-yah, ai-yah*" moaned up and down the long corridor through the rest of the sickening day and all night and the following days and nights. Horace and Neil worked over the men almost without stop. Ralph helped made traction frames and splints and Mary covered the splints. One Western trained Chinese doctor from South Side came part time to contribute his skill.

The battle appeared to be over. What had been settled by it? We did not know.

The next morning after my class at the college, I went to the hospital and offered my services. Horace looked at me with the "What can *you* do?" air. How I wished I had training!

"I have a strong stomach," I heard myself saying in spite of qualms. He relented, through desperation.

"Get some towels, then, and warm water. Let the men wash their faces. And try to clean the dried, caked blood from around their wounds. We haven't time."

I looked around for some equipment. Horace said, "The hospital coolies are heating water in their cooking quarters. Find a basin. Go up and ask Mary for ours.

Begin with those men at the end of the ward. We have to do a couple of amputations and some other surgery. Dr. Dyer is sending over her assistant while we operate."

As I hurried up the hill for supplies, I realized the difficulties. The handful of Chinese girls in training at Dr. Dyer's small women's hospital could not work with male patients…the old taboo. Her hospital was understaffed and overfull with bed patients, a large clinic, and always the maternity cases that were coming with increasing confidence to the Western hospital. There was still cholera in the city too. Chinese hospitals were nonexistent, and there were only three small mission hospitals for a city and countryside of half a million people. Due to a shortage of personnel, our men's hospital had closed its wards and most of its meager equipment had disappeared. However, enough wooden trestles and rattan pallets had been left so that the three coolies working as orderlies had got the men off the floor.

When I returned with my supplies, I found the water in the courtyard, in two Standard Oil tins, futilely attempting to heat over the three burners of an old oil stove that was spewing black smoke around the base of the tins. With a bamboo dipper, I filled my pitcher and returned to the ward.

Passing a small room used for surgery, I saw Horace and Neil by a table on which lay a man with two inches of jagged bone protruding from a leg wound, his foot just hanging.

Horace said, "Get out!" I knew his brusque manner was for my protection. The stench was sickening. I ran.

In the ward I filled a basin which I put on the floor, wrung out the small Turkish towel in the lukewarm water, and handed it with soap to the first patient, a thin, pocked man with a shoulder wound. To my surprise he welcomed this attention, and from then on it was easier. However, I discovered it was a long walk to the courtyard to empty the water and replenish. Also I realized the danger of spreading infections using the same towels and basin of water over and over. I found a bottle of Lysol and poured a generous amount into the basin.

The next man to whom I gave the towel exclaimed, "*Ai-ha*!" and let out a volley of what must have been full-flavored oaths. He sniffed the water, grimaced, and refused to use the towel. Thereafter I had to compromise with a few drops of Lysol and hope for the best.

Some of the men did not recover. Some were dismissed after minor injuries were treated. But there still remained some fifty badly injured men to be cared for.

For a week I went down daily to do what I could. Though their dialect was different, I recognized their words for thirst and for hunger. No translator was needed for the cry, "*Cing tiang-aah*—I hurt, I hurt!"

Now as I worked with them I began to feel a terrible pity—for so many were mere boys. Here was a round-faced fellow of about fifteen—a bullet had gone in behind his left eye and come out through his right cheek, miraculously missing his brain and eye muscles and doing no major injury. When he could see through his bandages, he smiled and joked in his strange dialect. To my delight, when I approached, he always offered some sly but good-natured remark that brought laughs from the patients able to laugh.

There was an emaciated little fellow just about to die from a bullet through his right lung. He watched for me, and as long as he had strength, called for water. It was the small-lost-boy look in his eyes—the wistful homesick look I could hardly stand.

Then there was the large man with an abdominal operation for a bullet who wasn't supposed to have water that night, but persuaded the orderly to give him a drink, perhaps the cause of his death. In the morning the orderly's answer to Horace was that it was better to die than be thirsty!

The first morning we sterilized the instruments at our house, and when I carried them into the surgery room, I saw a thumb sitting on a table. Later I saw the man to whom it belonged—a crabbed fat old soul who, when he found they couldn't put his thumb back on, wouldn't let the doctor dress his wound and insisted on leaving the hospital. With a chance of blood poisoning, Horace said.

In the ward from which the worst stench came was an older man whose arm had been shot through at the elbow. His constant "Tch, tch, tch… Tch, tch, tch" echoed across the ward. One of the wooden frames Ralph had improvised was put over him, and Dakin's solution dripped slowly onto the wound. Whenever I hear the words Dakin's solution, I see that crude frame, the man's hopeless face, his bone-exposed arm, and hear his repeated complaint. And I see Horace, his young face so fine and intense, working over him, using all his skill to save him. Finally he had to amputate. The man did not recover.

Neil and Dr. Li were pressed by their large daily clinic and could help with the soldiers only part-time.

In the evenings Horace returned to our home, and his language was not quotable in mission circles. How angry he was! Shaken not by the suffering and death, for he was used to that. And not too much by the lack of equipment, which handicapped him as a surgeon, for now he was used to that also. But infuriated by the needlessness of such man-made pointless butchery, the stupidity of a society that permitted it, a world that tolerated it and even fomented it, teaching men to be worse than beasts and with guns imported from western nations. For these men he was working over—these homeless mercenaries, the dregs, the *lowest* on the Chinese rung of society—still, they were human beings. And as a doctor he called on every ounce of his endurance and skill to help them. "To help them for what?" he asked bitterly.

Yet he kept on...sharing his rare skill with the able Chinese doctor at his side.

As for me, upset as a child unused to such experiences, the sights of the battle played over and over in my mind like a self-repeated reel. How cheap life was! How stupidly cruel! Was this China? Where was the beauty, the art, the culture? I don't know what I expected—but not this! Yet I knew what we had seen was only a tiny speck of horror compared to real war—those of the past, and the more terrible ones yet to come.

Slowly I realized that we were caught in something so much, *much* bigger than ourselves—that what we had seen was just a little surface symptom of China's deep, long sickness—and we knew we were helpless to change the great sweep of the forces of history in which we were all caught.

I am so useless, I thought. *What has happened to our dream?* As an antidote I tried to fix my thoughts on the students, for in them lay China's hopes.

Our house was so built that it had an outside door to Ralph's study, and there, some evenings, his students began to drop in. Some came out of curiosity, some for help. They liked to practice their English. And some were fascinated by a radio he was helping them build with a kit he had brought from America. Sometimes I joined them with a plate of cookies.

One boy, or young man, for these were upper high school students, older and more advanced in some ways than American students, talked about his country. His eloquent hands and flashing eyes filled in the gaps of his classroom English. He had been describing his view of the battle.

He said, "China suffers long enough. Our generation will make a better China. A great Lincoln Three-Principles-of-the-People Country, respect by all the world. But first we must become equal with the West. And we must have tools of West. Without tools of West we can do nothing!"

"The tools of the West?" I questioned, recalling the guns on the hillside. "Which tools?"

"Yes, which tools?" Ralph insisted quietly.

In China, it seems, things happen, and then later one learns why...or perhaps one never learns...

As to the battle, there were conflicting reports, but the most logical one was this:

The Old Foochow General and his "military" were not liked or trusted. Therefore the navy, which had its meager headquarters at Pagoda Anchorage and was supposed to help keep the peace, sent word to the Nationalist Government at Nanking for someone to come down and drive him out. So the 11th Army, the Invincible Iron Army, it was called, with its snappy young soldiers, was dispatched to Foochow.

Here it was welcomed with firecrackers and banners! The Foochow general went out to meet the New Iron Army general, and that evening, October 12, he and his officers were entertained by the New Iron Army general at a big feast—a reconciliation feast—"let's be friends and do this together" at the big yamen. Here some private money transactions took place that no one knew much about or how many thousands of dollars were handed over.

This accomplished, so the story went, the old general, after paying his "protection money," was captured in his own yamen by the new general and held with his officers. The next day, without warning, the Iron Army trained a couple of machine guns on the entrance to the old general's yamen and fired a few decoy rifle shots, which brought the Foochow soldiers running out. The machine guns firing at close range mowed down the old general's men. At the same time a group of soldiers chased another group from the yamen outside our gate, up Peace Street between our compound and the men's and women's hospitals. Later we saw the walls of Peace Street gouged, windows and gates pocked with holes, and the large pane of glass in the women's hospital shattered.

It was eventually reported that there were three to four hundred casualties, largely the old general's men—the ones who had been brought to our hospital. What happened to the old general we did not know. But now, under the new "military" we were all supposed to settle down and feel happy, knowing we were secure from attacks by Lu Ting Bang and/or other bandits!

That was China—winter of 1927-28.

Three weeks after the battle, Ralph and I took a walk. We went down the narrow lane past the small yamen to South Street. Dodging the load-bearers swinging by, we watched the long-coated merchants in their open shops; a young woman standing at the front of the Chinese-ink-and-paper stall jiggling her small son with big black eyes, and feeding him from a bowl with red chopsticks.

It was here where we had stood a year ago welcoming the Nationalist Army. It was this street through which we had hurried in the tiny horse-carriage nine months ago, caught in the angry mob attacking the Catholic orphanage. Here, in this street, we had been pulled in our rickshaws while soldiers were looting our compound and the foreign compounds of the city. It was through this street we had fled two days after that—destination Formosa.

I stayed close to Ralph as we wandered along, glancing in the shops, their entire fronts unboarded and open. Will this street ever be a friendly welcoming street? I wondered. Will it ever seem like home? Will we always be transplanted—"long-nose foreigners"? Always on the outside?

The busy merchants, used to Americans in this section, paid no attention. I relaxed. Noticing the inevitable posters on a wall, we went over to examine them. Here were two Chinese characters we had learned, derived from an ancient ideograph depicting a hand-throwing spear. "*Da do*—down with!" it shouted at us. The translation was now all too familiar to us: "Down with Imperialists! Down with Unequal Treaties!" And the new one, "Down with Communists!"

Odd that these posters should be here—just a five-minute walk from our hospital where for days we had watched the drama of healing. I looked at Ralph, and we laughed at the irony of it and tried to decipher the remaining characters.

But we understood. Anyone who knew the history of China could understand. We thought as we stood there—*it was a wonder we could stand there at all!*

Ralph said, nodding toward the hospital, "If a month from now those soldiers are led in some attack against foreigners, under whatever bandit or general, they won't distinguish. Our sins are collective. We all wear the same white face."

"I don't believe it!" I was cross with Ralph for being so objective. "If any of those men saw Horace again, they'd try to protect him. If not, what are we here for?"

"To do the best we can—regardless of the outcome. You know that." He smiled down at me, and for a minute, we were alone in the middle of that Chinese street.

Ralph believed this so implicitly he never was afraid…not in any of the hazards we were yet to face. Sometimes I wished he would be…just a little! But I longed for courage to match his.

A few weeks after this, something happened that both increased my ability to be apprehensive and added a whole exciting dimension to our lives.

On an unusually warm morning for January, taking advantage of the sunshine, I was on the porch with my Chinese teacher repeating phrases from our Foochow phrase book. My mind wandered. We had been too well initiated into some of China's miseries, I thought. If only now we could experience some of the better aspects, get to know some people of the upper classes—the teachers in our college, to experience some of the culture we had read about…

Suddenly I felt ill and ran into the house.

When I returned, Grandpa Ding smiled and with customary Chinese naturalness said, "The Sinaniong is gong to '*iong giang*'—to have a child, *iong* meaning to bring forth with effort, and *giang*, of course, is child, or 'small thing.' Also friends will offer you the congratulatory wish..." And he told me the Chinese expression, which might be translated, "May it be a beautiful boy!"

He said, "Repeat it now after me." And he said it again, and a second time and a third, till I caught the tones and rhythm. *Ah, the music of this language!*

I laughed and repeated it. What a beautiful expression! Suddenly I realized that a Chinese phrase had acquired for the first time, for me, a real and wonderful meaning.

After this, Grandpa Ding explained the origin of the Chinese characters I was learning to write awkwardly with brush and black Chinese ink ground on an ink slab. He told me about the Chinese dragon, and the Feast of Lanterns, the New Year customs, ancestors, and why sons were so important to every Chinese family.

"Son or daughter," I said to myself, practicing the Chinese words. It didn't matter to me. Secretly I thought a girl for the *first* one would be nice. But I didn't dare admit that to Grandpa Ding.

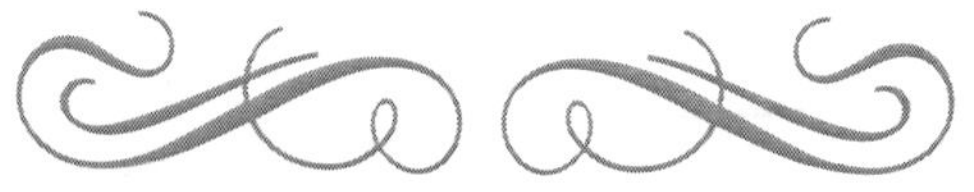

Dragon Dance

February 1928

Talkie-True, the curio man, grinned. Carefully he set down his Chinese baskets. Competing with Grandpa Ding for my language study time, he squatted for the third time that week on our porch and spread his embroideries, bowls, and scrolls.

"This veree old, missy." He slid the top from a wooden box and with reverent fingers held up a bowl with carved stand and cover. Blue dragons romped around the delicate white porcelain. "See, one piece belong emperor. A-numbah-one. Five-toe dragon…Chi'en Lung Dynasty."

He unfolded an enormous blue and gold Mandarin coat. "*Kossu*, cut silk. *Si-sik*, truly-truly, this coat veree old. Belong emperor. See five-toe dragon. I talkee-true."

Next the curio man produced a dragon scroll. Yielding, I bargained with him for the bowl and he went away still grinning.

Grandpa Ding had been watching, and beneath his noncommittal expression, I sensed amusement.

"It is *si-sik* a Chi'en Lung piece?"

He gave the bowl careful scrutiny. "Perhaps *si-sik*... perhaps copy. Has five-toe dragon." His old eyes lighted.

"You'll see real dragon soon."

"The real thing?" Was he teasing me?

"Yes, he will dance on the hill." I thought, that Chinese dragon—you can't go anywhere without bumping into him—stumbling over, being drowned by, threatened by or protected by one of his kind. He was everywhere! Sometimes beneficial. Sometimes troublesome. But always a potent presence.

One night standing on our hill under the stars, watching the earth's shadow take a bite from the moon, we had heard a loud commotion from the streets below—shouts, brass cymbals banging. Voices raised in fear. The people were crying, "*Loong* (Dragon), go away! Go! Don't swallow our moon!"

As the dark bite grew, the roar increased. Then the shadow hesitated, paused. The voices cried, "Look! The shadow leaves. We have frightened *Loong* away. We have saved our moon!" The roar turned to shouts of joy, and we, too, cheered.

Another time, crossing the Formosa channel, our boat tossing like a corked bottle, the captain pointed to the jagged mountains we were leaving. "Two dragons fight, long time ago... toss up island of Formosa." Then he pointed and told us that at the bottom of the channel lived a monster who, thrashing his angry tail, churned the sea into the roughest white water of any channel in the world. It seemed entirely possible.

I asked Grandpa Ding, "Where did the dragon come from?"

"He is as old as memory." The teacher, twisting his sparse whiskers, quoted the most ancient of Chinese classics, the *I Ching*.

"A mighty monster arose from a river in Honan and appeared to the ruler Fsu His. This was in 2962 BC as you reckon time." The old man's supple hands moved to emphasize his purposely slow Chinese words. "*Loong* can do many things: shorten or lengthen himself at will, make himself dark or luminous, thin or heavy. There are many kinds: heavenly dragons, earthly dragons that control the winds and clouds and rain. The dragon of the hidden treasure watches over the wealth hidden from mortals; and the Imperial dragon with the fifth claw is associated only with the Son of Heaven, the emperor."

We knew... We had heard the dragon's roar in the typhoons that swept up from the south. Heat lightening streaking across the sky was his forked tongue. His breath came in puffs from the sea and gathered on the mountain ranges in trails of mist. His frozen breath fell in snowflakes, but so rarely in the southern hills that it was gathered and packed in tins and sold in the city streets as potent magic.

Loong, Grandpa Ding told me, was always waiting in the angry currents of the river, and if a man fell in, no one would be foolish enough to rescue him for that would rob the river spirit of his prey and anger him to revenge. Sometimes a playful dragon romped with children, tugging kites high into the whipping winds. In summer when the sun burned hot day after day, and men pulled weeds for food, they knew the dragon was angry and lighted incense at small shrines. When at last welcome clouds mounted in the copper sky and loosed healing rains, the people knew their fragrant prayers curling upward had reached him—good had triumphed over evil. A friendly dragon!

"Tell me about *our* dragon," I said to Grandpa Ding, recalling he had told me that we had one in our own compound, and I pointed to the mound of ivy-covered rock shaded by a very old banyan tree.

"But he is not *your* dragon. He belongs to the city of Foochow. That rock, called Golden Platform, pins down the dragon-guardian of the city. When the foreigners bought this land, the Chinese city fathers would not sell the rock. They thought if the barbarians owned the spirit this would anger him and upset the Wind and Water influence and harm the city. This is Chinese geomancy."

I felt glad that we did not own the rock.

"You'll see him soon," the teacher repeated, his face alight as he pointed to the temples visible high on the hill beyond our wall. "He'll dance there in the Chinese New Year."

Did Grandpa Ding believe in the dragon? I could not tell, but as he talked he made me believe.

Soon we would see the dragon in person. I could hardly wait…

On a late afternoon we climbed the hill, and there before a small temple in the midst of a boisterous crowd we saw him.

There, from the pages of legend, lighted by the setting sun, the huge creature moved in flowing curves, his long body undulating in true dragon waves and coiling circles. His tail lashed. His giant head shook from side to side. He blinked his protruding eyes. He snapped his sharp toothed jaws open and shut, and real flame shot out with his darting red tongue. Smoke poured from his wide snorting nostrils.

Ahead of him, elusive, tantalizing, danced a round white orb, the Pearl. The sun? The moon? The earth? Symbol of immortality? Whatever it was, the dragon could never catch it. As he opened his mouth close upon his prey, the crowd roared spurring the Pearl to leap ahead barely escaping the jaws and flame. Around, in and out, Dragon ran, surging into the people, making them draw back clutching each other with cries of delighted terror.

Soon we discovered all this was merely rehearsal.

Darkness fell. The dragon rested. Suddenly we saw hundreds of candles glowing in the temple backdrop. This was our cue to light the small paper lanterns of every conceivable shape that we and the others carried. At the same time we watched some twenty pairs of human feet attached to men emerge from under the reptile's body. This was made, we surmised, of a bamboo frame with poles inside to manipulate it, the whole hundred-foot length covered with white cloth and multi-colored scales.

The grimacing face, enhanced by tentacles, horny brows and mane, fangs and claws of intricate workmanship, gave the creature an air of awesome splendor…and gorgeous make-believe.

Now the length of the dragon's body was illumined from within, and a light glowed from the Pearl. I watched as a path was cleared through the crowd, and Pearl, Dragon, and lanterns wound down the hill.

In the city along the crowded main street the people were waiting impatiently. They welcomed the dragon with pounding drums and banging firecrackers. I could smell the sharp smoke and feel the explosions in the narrow street. Moving forward, again the Dragon danced—he undulated, he darted from side to side shaking his head. Fire spit from his mouth, leaping against the darkness, lighting the faces of the enthralled watchers, while cymbals crashed and shouts rose above the rooftops.

What a spectacle…what a festival!

As we followed, our own small lanterns bobbing on bamboo sticks, we were caught into another world—something elemental, this drama out of the misty past, out of the roots of life…these ancient rhythms, supplications… symbol of the battle of storm and sun, darkness and light, the eternal conflict of evil and goodness.

Dragon—loong, the cymbals and shouts cried, *don't be our enemy! Be our friend. Bring us food. Drive away evil. Conquer darkness. Don't swallow our moon. Don't destroy our earth! Never devour our Pearl…our hope…our immortality!*

With excitement and foreboding, I recalled the saying attributed to Napoleon, "China is a sleeping dragon. When she wakens, she will shake the world."

But this was a benevolent dragon. And in the dark street the lighted Pearl continued to leap and dance ahead, unharmed.

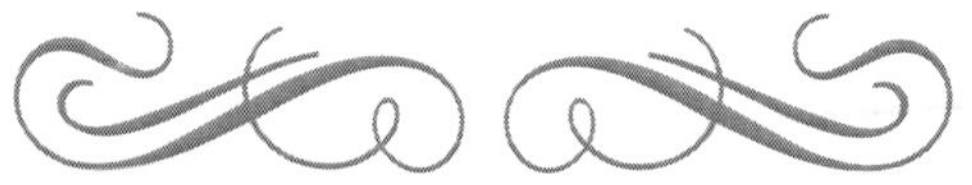

Walls

February 1928

Walls. Walls around cities, walls around homes, around temples…around the pagoda, even around the hospital, walls for fire protection separating crowded wooden dwellings in the city. The wall around our compound of American homes! I could understand walls in China better after the battle. But this wall running beside our garden and lawn, bisecting our hill—this ten foot high wall covered along the top with broken glass embedded in the cement—this wall bisected our lives, cut us off from the students on the other side. *How stupid,* I thought. *Let's break it down!*

A few feet from our front walk was the small gate through the wall, but the gate must be kept locked at all times. To be sure Ralph had a key, but only to let himself through when going to classes.

It was February 1928. Outside, I could tell, the night was sparkling cold. I felt the cold creeping in through the floors and walls of our unheated house built for semitropics. The large living room was full of cold shadows.

"Let's have a fire in the fireplace," I said to Ralph.

"Or get some clothes on," he said, grinning at the blanket I'd wrapped around me. We'll build a little fire in the study." This was a concession, coal being so impossibly expensive.

Just then we heard something—a shuffling sound and low voices. The brass knocker tapped on the front door, and again…hard. Was it angry? Or just impatient?

Ralph strode across and opened the door wide. The porch was crowded with students. Students? We'd been advised not to have them in as a group—the antiforeign feeling, secret cells, threats. But here they were—a porch full of them, in their long cotton winter-padded coats.

Students! Ralph's students. I thought… Oh, come in! Glancing at Ralph for a clue, I could tell he was as surprised as I.

"Come in," he said then urged it again in Chinese.

In the semidark of the porch, I saw the boys turn their eyes like a chorus to a tall, stern young man in their midst. "Speak up," their eyes said to him.

The leader held his head high. He did not incline it, in the Chinese custom, before his teacher. My heart jumped. What was wrong? This was not as I had imagined it.

"Won't you come in?"

No one moved. The many eyes prodded their leader—*go on, speak.* He cleared his throat.

"Choi Sinang (Shrader, Teacher), next week is examination." His groping English sounds like memorized speech. "We will talk to you. Give us no examination on text book."

It was an order—this blunt demand. And from students! What had happened to the polite talk that always preceded negotiations? Or was it language that was the barrier?

If Ralph was annoyed or amused, he didn't show it. He looked at them deliberately, considering. "This seems a strange request. Is it…the *custom*?"

The students stared at him and at one another. The custom? One nodded and was nudged to silence. Ralph said, "Tell me, who sent you?"

The leader said, "No one sent. It is class wish. We are a…a…"

"Delegation?"

"Yes, delegation."

"Tell me, what do you want?" Ralph smiled warmly. "Don't be afraid. What do you really want?" He looked around. "Sui-ing? Dai-hok?"

Now several spoke at once. "The rules—the rules in the book. Too hard. We cannot understand."

Ralph said, "I'm afraid I don't understand you. Wouldn't it be better if you came in? It's cold out here."

The spokesman did not move, but a shove from the rear pushed him forward and they all came crowding in. Ralph gave me a nod toward the kitchen, and I ran down the hall.

"Huo-seng, cookies and tea." But the kitchen was dark and the charcoal fire dead. I could not ask for hot water now. Huo-seng had gone to his quarters below. I found the square tin. Ah, some ginger cookies. I arranged them on a plate and returned to the living room where the boys were seated now on the wicker settee, chairs, and floor… the cold floor. I longed to build a fire. But in their padded coats, I hope they do not notice. Their dormitories and classrooms are never heated, I remembered.

I passed the cookies. The boys looked up smiling at me.

"*Sia-sia*, thank you. Don't trouble yourself."

The leader ignored the cookie plate. He was speaking in Chinese to the others. I noticed his thin, scornful face, his hair cut in the extreme modern fashion, long to the neck. These boys seemed all older, more mature than American students of similar age. And this one appeared to be older than the rest—a self-appointed leader? They grew quiet, listening to his rapid words spoken in undertones, watching his eyes. They nodded approval at last, forgetting the cookies they were still munching. That was what he wanted. He jumped up and faced Ralph. His eyes were blackly defiant.

"Choi Sinang, I speak to you for students."

Ralph, standing behind the large wicker chair, said easily, "Go ahead. I am listening."

"Choi Sinang, the times are very trouble. Students have many problems. Much work to do for country. Now examination time. If you must give examination, we ask… no rules from book."

"And what would *you* suggest I ask you in the examination?"

There was a pause as the boys looked at each other. One with a round, roguish face looked at Ralph hesitantly, Ralph nodded, and the boy stood, grinning broadly. "May I speak?" As if a playful wind had brushed against them, the tense faces relaxed into half smiles. This must be the class "clown" Ralph had mentioned.

"Yes, Ding-chung."

"If we were teacher, we would not give examination at all."

They laugh and applaud. Like puppets, I thought, to be moved one way or the other. But they were watching their teacher. At his smile they all began to talk. Their eagerness spilled over into broken phrases. "We will write for you…story of my life…a short story…but no rules… no rules…"

A young-looking boy with bright eyes and sensitive face raised his hand.

"Yes, Siu-ing?"

"Choi Sinang, I suggest you give us question—to write a thought from our thinking."

Ralph sat down in the big chair as the English and Chinese words mingled with the cookies they were finishing. At last, when the plate was emptied, he addressed them.

"Now I will speak to you."They were silently watching him. "Thoughts from your thinking, Siu-ing suggested. Yes, that is what I would like to have. Soon. But now we study composition. The bones to build your thoughts around. Tell me, is there anyone here who is ambitious?

Who plans to continue his work at the university after he has graduated here?"

The sudden switch surprised them. Several raised hands, then they all said…yes, yes…of course…

"Why? Why go to school for four more years?"

They turn to each other and talk in Chinese.

"Tell me in English," Ralph insisted.

"We must…our country needs…prepare…"

"Why?"

"China is great country…must make strong government…overthrow opposition…drive out western powers…China for Chinese…too much corruption…make honest leaders…no, make strong leaders…"

The spokesman watched the others, his lips drawn tight. I imagined him on a crowded corner stirring up a crowd. Suddenly he stood up.

"You waste time. This is not purpose of visit." His words fell like heavy slaps across the eagerness in the faces of the others. He turned to Ralph. "I will speak once more now for class. We come to house of teacher to say—do not make us to study textbook before examination. Do not make questions on book."

The moment of intimacy was broken. Now the boys remembered the purpose of their visit. They looked at Ralph hopefully…or was it fearfully? They have defied custom by confronting a teacher in this way. They could be in serious trouble for this. Or *we* could.

There is a contest going on here, I thought. Not a noisy one like the battle…not yet. But a battle nevertheless.

What will Ralph do? I saw him playing for time as he rose deliberately and took his stand behind his chair, his face taut. *What a razor-edge a teacher has to walk these days*, I thought. Especially one who has come not to "just teach"...but to work *with*...to try to understand. The old days are gone—the revered elder-scholar, and his students bowing from the waist. How can a teacher today balance on that edge between friendship and respect? Between the desire to reach out and touch a heart or mind, and to maintain discipline?

I could almost see the slogans running through their minds—*huang-giang*, foreigner. This goes deeper than the age-old student-teacher struggle. This is a struggle between East and West—fruit of a Hundred Years' War.

Which side of the razor edge will Ralph take? I wonder. *Here in this room is what we have come to China for.* But how different from the dream. All these young men, defiant, were staring at Ralph with their bright, dark eyes. All of them testing him, trying to push him, to bend him to their will, to win. And these, I know, are but a segment of a city-wide, nation-wide youth, proud, impatient, burning with patriotism.

Don't be a huang-giang—a foreigner! I think to Ralph. *Don't drive them farther away. We'll lose our chance.*

Ralph came slowly from behind his chair. I could see the students scarcely breathing as they waited for his answer. His voice was strong, serious.

"Three years from now, if you pass, you will be taking exams for the university. Siu-ing, you suggested 'thoughts from your thinking.' In the examination I *will* ask you some thoughts, on different subjects. They matter...for your country. Perhaps they matter for the world." Ah... the boys breathe... "And *if*, listen, I say *if* you think you can pass the examination without further study of our textbook, it will be perfectly all right with me."

The boys looked at each other...what kind of answer was this? Ding-chung, the clown gave the cue, grinned. "*Hao hao*, good. It is good."

They relaxed. They smiled. A bargain, a meeting ground. Some even laughed. They have not won, but neither have they lost completely. They have not been made to lose face.

"It is *our* choice—-what he says has reason." They repeated in Chinese, "*O li, o li.*"

They rose and moved, a little reluctantly it seemed to me, to the door and out to the porch. Ralph glanced at the locked gate in the wall by our garden. "How did you get in here to our house?"

They gestured in the opposite direction. "We came the long way around. Of course. This gate is always locked."

Ralph said, "Wait," and fumbled in his pocket for the large key. They walked together to the gate. It creaked open and they filed through. "Next time send a messenger, let me know ahead, and I will open it." As they started down the stone steps, he called the courtesy phrase in Chinese, "Slowly-slowly-walk."

"We make you too much trouble...go within," they replied in self-conscious English, grinning. Only the leader did not respond. He stalked down the steps looking straight ahead.

"Come again," we called in Chinese. "Come again!"

Back in the living room, we straightened the chairs. It no longer seemed cold.

"What's the name of their leader?" I asked.

"Huo-hok. I hardly know him. He entered very late."

I tried to recall. "Huo…harmony. Hok…happy. Happy Harmony…well!

"My guess is," said Ralph, "that we haven't heard the last of him."

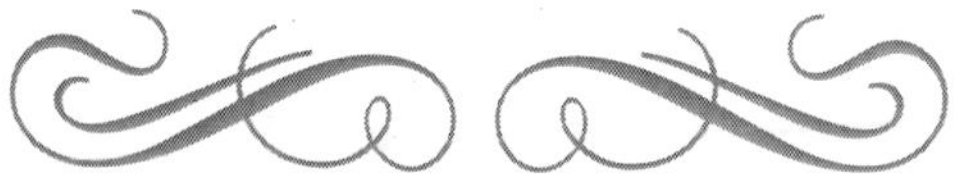

The College Burns

February 1928

The day the Chens, Snow-Gold and Ciu Ding (Robert was his American name), were coming to our house to dinner, an incident occurred which helped us understand the seriousness, even danger, of their situation.

It was a cold February day during the Chinese New Year vacation. Ralph came back from the almost deserted college and tossed on my desk a sheet of yellow paper covered with Chinese characters. "What do you think of this?" he asked.

I looked at it puzzled. "Are you kidding? Read it!"

"Just a bit of propaganda—strewn all over the college campus. Translation on the back. I got the dean to translate it for me. Reluctantly."

"I think the Chinese teachers aren't happy about telling us what the antiforeign line puts out. They're too courteous." Turning over the paper, I read the following:

> "Let there be a wave of voices crying, 'Down with the Christian Schools.' Already the cry

> has ascended to heaven. You Christian school dogs—you have not served your country's revolution. You have privately and insidiously tried to destroy your country. You are the revolution's most sinful men. You are the Party's greatest hindrance."
>
> "Students of the Christian schools, you have been denationalized."
>
> "If you do not wake up you are not citizens."
>
> "Wake up! Wake up quickly!"
>
> "Turn back to your country!"
>
> "Down with every Christian school!"

I handed back the sheet. "They're really getting hot! Is this the hand of Happy Harmony?"

Ralph said, "The trouble is, it's such a mixture of truth and blindness. And contradiction. The radicals hate the West but want all the things the West has to offer. They get confused."

"What did the Dean say?"

"He tried to soften the blow by assuring me that these radical groups are frequently made up of students who have failed and are disgruntled. They are a minority. However, some are terribly sincere and dedicated."

"They express themselves rather forcefully," I commented and went about preparations for dinner. I so wanted it to be a good evening.

Ralph and I were excited about the Chens' return to Foochow. We had looked forward to their coming ever since the day a year ago at Pagoda Anchorage, at the tensely contested meeting, when it was decided that the top positions in all our schools would be turned over to the Chinese.

Robert and Snow-Gold were studying then at Columbia University. Robert accepted the offer to be the new *hau-ciong*, principal of Foochow College. This was as it should be.

Since the founding in 1853 of the school, a boarding school for boys, and the first of its kind in that province, it had grown from a primary school to a college of several departments, somewhat on the English plan. It provided the highest education, Western style, for boys in the entire province, until the establishment of the Fukien Christian University. After that Foochow College maintained the reputation for the best preparatory education available for boys. It had more applications than it could handle, the upper-class Chinese families, Christian or not, recognized its standards. They were aware of the need for this type of education in their country as it now tried to take its place with western nations. It had an excellent staff of Chinese faculty, and taught Chinese subjects as well as western, so the students carried a double load.

Now, for the first time in its history, the main teacher sent out from America by the American Board, instead of being the principal of the college, would work under the direction of a Chinese administrator. To us this seemed exactly right. It was the work Ralph had chosen and been chosen for. We so wanted this new relationship to be successful—for the sake of the college and all it stood for in South China—and for the sake of Robert and Snow-Gold, pioneering in such different times in their own home city.

Impatiently we had looked forward to their coming. Now they were here in time to prepare for the opening of the second term. When we met them the day of their arrival, we were surprised to see Robert so young looking. I thought he looks almost like one of the students—so slender and eager. His sensitive finely shaped face was open and clear-eyed, friendly. His assured poise gave him the necessary maturity. He was completely at ease, we observed, as he greeted his old friends. Snow-Gold, too, we liked. In contrast to Robert, she was strongly built, her broad features not pretty like so many of the Chinese girls, but when she smiled it was as though her whole face, her eyes, had lighted from within. I thought, she has courage that woman, and a very good mind. She will need both. At once I admired her and envied her.

When we were introduced, Robert shook Ralph's hand in the western fashion, warmly, and smiled with complete pleasure.

Robert said, "You are to be our coworkers!"

In this way we joined forces.

It was a good thing we had seen that yellow sheet, for it gave us background for what Robert had to tell us when they came to have dinner alone with us that evening.

After the meal, and after making sure that E-song had left the room and the door to the kitchen was closed, Robert pulled out a letter, scrutinizing it carefully under the dim lights of our dining room. He frowned, his fine face looking troubled.

"Listen to this. It came in the mail yesterday. I haven't mentioned it to anyone. Maybe I shouldn't..." Then he read: "Running dog of the foreigners...if you become the president of this college we will kill you and burn your buildings...do not be the tool of imperialism...do not betray the revolution!"

As he read, my heart tightened. I thought, *Now it's really coming close!*

He looked up. "Should I toss it out and forget it?"

Snow-Gold looked from Robert to us, the light accenting her strong features. Half-smiling, she said, "A friendly welcome, isn't it?"

"May I see it?" asked Ralph. I examined it with him. "Was it written by a student?" It was pencil scrawled on notebook paper, in Chinese characters with the English words written below.

"It's hard to tell," said Robert. "The extremists of any group love to do this sort of thing."

Snow-Gold said, "It could be. You know how excited the students are, and the pressure of the propaganda. There may easily be some Communist sympathizers in the school. You remember the fire four months ago? We think it was an inside job."

Indeed I remembered the fire, it came soon after the battle. Under extreme difficulties the college continued. There was no proof of guilt established. It was the times—the revolution. The majority of students were loyal to the new government and the school. The trouble was to know who was friend and who was not.

Snow-Gold said, with a wry smile, "Dr. Ling thinks Robert should have a bodyguard. Just a couple of Secret Service men. He has to go through the streets so much. I told him at the rate he moves no bodyguard could possible keep up with him!"

"Robert," said Ralph "you know, I don't think that's too bad an idea."

Ralph handed the letter back to Robert who stuffed it in his pocket. We were all thoughtful as he said slowly, "It's not me I'm concerned about. I don't think they'd dare make an attempt on my life—I'm not worth the risk." He smiled at Snow-Gold across the table.

Robert continued, "It's not myself—it's the college. We can't afford to lose more buildings. Not only a matter of space, which is already a problem. But morale. What would it do to the rest of the students who are so easily and so definitely associated with the foreigners—you imperialists? He grinned. "I wonder if this is the time for us to take the leadership…perhaps we should wait…"

Ralph broke in, "No…no. We've waited too long already. The question is…should we be here…at all…"

There was quiet for a few minutes, all of us trying to see into the question…into the future. Ralph reminded Robert that there were over forty Chinese in Foochow who had come back recently with their higher degrees from abroad. Robert said quietly, "I will need *you*. Our worlds are meeting…it's a joint enterprise. I will *need* you."

Later, when the Chens were leaving, Ralph returned to the matter of the bodyguard. "You'd better settle for that."

Robert shrugged. "If they're going to shoot me they'll shoot me. But I don't think they'll try. They don't want to get executed. It's the college buildings I'm worried about—I'd hate to think our presence here might cause more damage."

"How about a bodyguard for the school?" Ralph was not joking.

"I've requested an additional watchman," Robert replied.

When they had gone, I looked toward the wall at the left, visualizing the dark and deserted college grounds below. I was glad for the night watchman who made his rounds, announcing the hour on his hollow bamboo rattle.

On the following Sunday evening, the day after the return of the students for the spring term, E-song came pushing open the swinging door to the dining-room, waving his arm toward the college and shouting, "*Hui*! *Hui*!" The school is on fire! Scientific Institute has fire!

We rushed to the porch. About one hundred feet from our home, beyond the low college wall, we could see black smoke pouring out of the dormitory roof slightly below the level of our home. As we ran along the walk and pulled open the small gate in the wall, we could hear shouts. Below we saw the courtyard in confusion. Students, their long blue coats flopping about their ankles, were running from the door of the burning building, carrying bed quilts, clothes, and books. Other students were bumping into them as they tried to get into the building. Hurrying down the stone steps, we saw the flames shooting, hissing through the roof and windows of the dormitory to our left. Window glass cracked and fell, smashing loudly on the stone below.

As we neared the bottom step, we saw Robert disappearing into a side door of the science wing away from the fire. In a minute he reappeared calling students and pointing. "The lab equipment. Get the lab equipment out." They flocked in and came back, each carrying some fragile and precious piece—jars of chemicals, microscopes, glass apparatus, which they set down nearby and then ran in for more.

As we started to follow, there came from behind us another sound. Above the crackling of the flames and roar of burning wood, we heard the crash of cymbals and pop-bang, pop-bang of large firecrackers. *What now?* I thought, *as if we didn't have enough*! I looked across the court to the big college gate. Aaah! At last…the fire department! Now we would have help… The dormitory, burning wildly, couldn't be saved. But what about the wing—maybe the science wing…if they hurried.

Pushed back now by the intense heat that leaped toward us heating our face, our noses stung by the acrid smell, we stood helplessly watching. Robert was shoving the students back out of range of falling, burning wood. Now we saw the firemen, in glorious uniform, march across the court. The leader wore a high steel helmet with an eagle perched on top, and in his hand he carried a long bamboo pole with a huge Chinese lantern, characters inscribed, about four feet high bobbing from the top of the pole. Deliberately, calmly, he surveyed the burning building, then blew a blast on his whistle. Two blasts.

The crowd drew back. As the firemen approached we could see their uniforms of scarlet or yellow emblazoned with dragons and other symbols. Surrounding these important men were lesser men in black carrying small lanterns on sticks, differing in design for the different platoons. Others of the company beat brass cymbals or set off firecrackers. Still others simply shouted, again and again, their faces a mixture of delight and terror.

A leader of each platoon, at a command from the head man, marked off his section of the fire he was to control and stationed his firemen and noise-makers. *Hurry!* I thought. *Hurry!* They were so deliberate.

Then at last—action! One platoon marched to the nearest well about thirty feet away, pulled off the lid and peered in. Water? Water? A bucket brigade approached and a bucket was lowered. It came up half full. All right then—a bucket line. And the line formed from the well to the fire-wagon. This was an oblong tank mounted on little wheels that had been pulled by a dozen straining coolies to the front of the building. Now the filled buckets passed from man to man, like an endless chain, dumping the water with a splash into the water tank and returning the emptied buckets back down another line.

Four men mounted the hand pump on the tank, and we could hear under the crackling flames their rhythmic "Uh, huh; uh, huh," as they pulled the heavy pump handle back and forth. When at last a feeble stream of water about twelve feet high shot from the hose, a cheer rose from the crowd. By now the hot, growing, fire was spreading down into the rooms on the ground level, and we could hear a hissing as the water reached into the flames like a weak and wavering finger…the mounting terrifying flames and that little water!

Another bucket brigade formed a second line from a second well. This augmented the water, which was directed now toward the protection of the wing. Fresh pumpers leaped to the pump.

The cymbals crashed faster and faster, beaten furiously by the men whose duty it was to frighten off the fire-dragon. Firecrackers exploded. All this in the dancing black shadows and red light—like the famous temple wall scene depicting the tortures of hell.

The crowd gasped as each new burst of sparks shot high above us, and charred beams tore loose and fell.

Pointing upward, someone in the crowd cried, "The wall, the wall!" and the people cringed back while part of the roof caved in and the upper part of the brick wall slid with a roar and flying debris to the ground. It sounded like the roar of the dragon, and it seemed that I could see his coiling red fury and snorting black puffs of angry breath mounting into the evening sky. Fight the dragon off, I begged. Frighten him away! Don't let him destroy the wing of the building too!

Then the rain started to fall.

Eyes looked up. Rain—the enemy of the fire dragon... *Ai-ha! Ai-ha!*

Ralph and I moved over to Robert and Snow-Gold who was close beside him. I saw their faces, drawn in the eerie light, tense with misery and anger. What a painful experience, I thought, to a couple just back from Columbia—how hurtful to pride as well as dreams. Then I remembered it had not been many years, relative to history, since we'd been pumping water by hand on our fires in America, without even the glory of brass cymbals and dragons.

I looked at Robert and saw that he was not conscious of the tears that ran down his cheeks. And I heard him murmur, like a groan, "They don't know what they're doing...they don't know..."

Then Snow-Gold said grimly, "We'll build again. You wait and see. We'll do it. We have to!"

The rain fell and the wind shifted the flames away from the wing. At last, relieved but heavy hearted, we climbed the steps back to our house. Then we noticed students also climbing the steps carrying apparatus from the laboratory. The gate was open and we met a string of students coming down the walk from our house. Some of them we knew—Sin-ding, Dai-hok, and yes, Happy Harmony!

One bowed slightly and said in English, "Sinang—Teacher—we have taken courage to place science equipment on your house. We hope that will be favorable to you."

Ralph assured them it was favorable. The student continued, "Will be more. Chemicals can explode in too great heat. Microscopes can spoil in rain."

"Bring them," Ralph said.

On the porch Mary welcomed us. "Horace is at the hospital treating some burns. Nothing serious. When I saw the sparks blowing on our roof and the chemicals arriving, I thought it was time to move Jane out. I carried her to Dr. Dyer's."

"I think it's safe to return her now," I said, but we both eyed the rows of chemicals in their glass bottles dubiously.

Later, very late judging by our exhaustion, we were ready for bed when Mary came running from her front room to ours at the back.

She called, "Come—look what I see!"

We looked. In the darkness we saw the four-foot lantern bobbing along in front of our house, and behind it a long procession of small lighted lanterns with their different emblems. We assumed there were feet under them. Then the lanterns stopped and waited. They continued to wait.

"What do they want?" we asked each other.

Lights flicked on at the Leger house, and we saw Mr. Leger, pajama clad, come out and enter into conversation with the big lantern. Then he came to us.

"It's the custom for the host and hostess of the fire to serve the brigade tea. I guess we'll have to get the kettles on."

We groaned. Kettles meant Standard Oil tins of water on a now cold charcoal stove. It was a process—the hard charcoal, the kindling paper, the wood shavings, the fanning, the smoke in our eyes, and the long wait for the large tins of water to heat. It was distinctly a cook's job.

As head of the domestic department, I recognized my responsibility. But Huo-seng? This time of night? I quailed and looked at the lanterns wishing fervently they would go home. The lights wavered, I thought, a trifle impatiently. I feared a serious rupture with my "Lord of the Kitchen." Slowly I walked down the long hall to the rear, thinking I would have to go downstairs to his room and waken him. But look! Could it be: a light under the closed kitchen door? I pushed it open.

"Huo-seng." I gasped, my heart rising to bless him. "Tea?"

He was waving his stove-fan before red coals on which stood three large tins, steam rising from them.

He said, "Al-light, al-light. Almost ready. I will take it to them. Get your sleep."

"You knew?"

"Of course. It is the custom, tea after the fire."

Tea disposed of, we watched the lanterns with their dragons bob out the gate and down the steps the way they had come. And then we heard the night watchman click the bar of the gate into place as he made his night rounds, and shake his hollow bamboo rattle sounding the hour. It was the custom, I thought, comforted.

During the coming spring months of 1928, from our porch we could hear a different sound—the sound of building...creaking wheelbarrows, pounding and hammering of carpenters, shouts of brick layers and masons.

The college was forced to close for the term, but Robert and Snow-Gold, with small assistance from America, worked endlessly to secure funds, and to carry through the difficult task of erecting modern buildings in a country without machines—the tools of the West.

With the heat of the summer months coming, and the fact that I was six months pregnant, we rented a small cottage at Kuliang in the mountains.

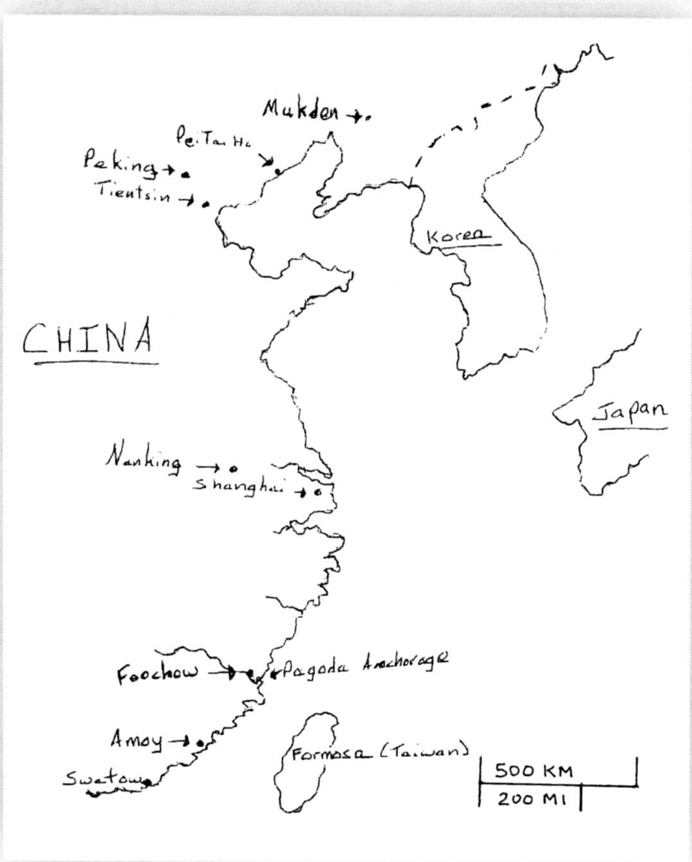

Southeast China, Courtesy of Jana L. Jackson

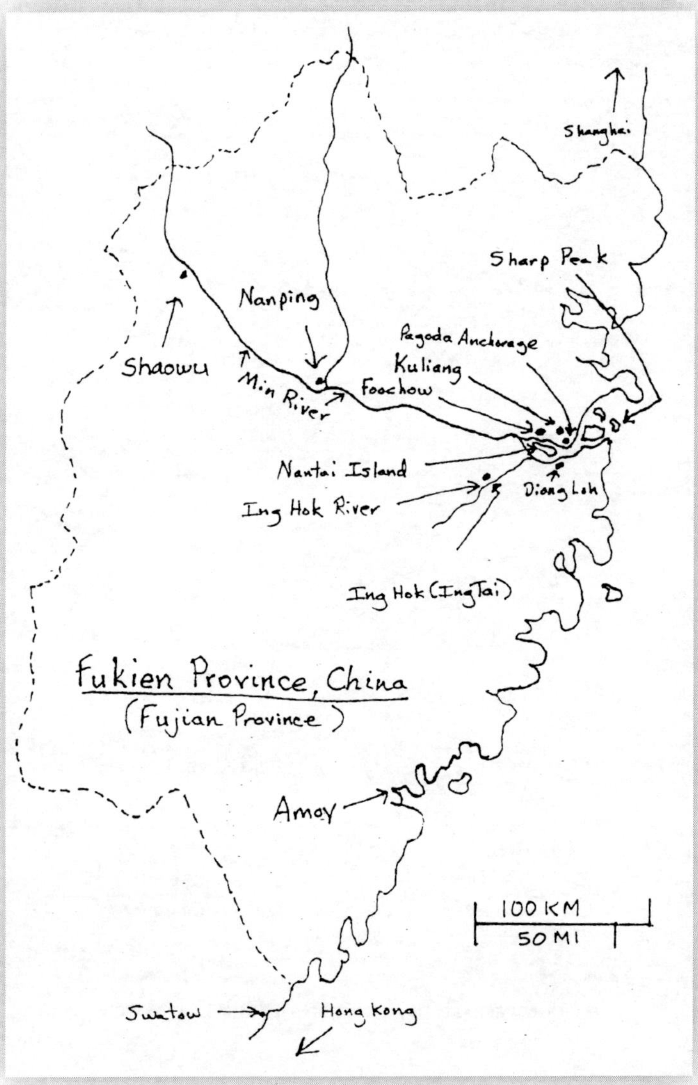

Fukien Province, Courtesy of Jana L. Jackson

White Pagoda

White Pagoda Seen through our Front Door

Our house in the Compound of American Homes. Amah is in the doorway with Whitney and Ka-trine is on the Lawn. I am leaning over checking on everybody.

The presence of gunboats of the Western nations was part of the pressure used to force China to accept the Unequal Treaties. They were also used to enforce the Unequal Treaties. These tactics have been referred to as Gunboat Diplomacy.

A typical Sampan is shown on the Min River near Foochow

I am in the Bamboo Chair about to descend from Kuliang to Foochow to give birth to Ka-trine. Ralph is standing behind me.

The Students of Foochow College. Ralph is fifth from left. The Chinese principal, Ciu Ding (Robert) is the Leftmost Seated.

Whitney, Ka-trine, and Myself in front of our house in the spring of 1931.

Front of the farewell card from the senior students shortly before our departure in the spring of 1932.

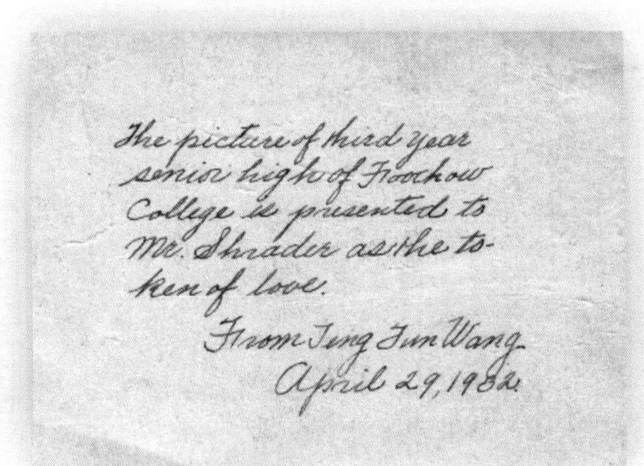

The picture of third year senior high of Foochow College is presented to Mr. Shrader as the token of love.

From Tung Tun Wang.
April 29, 1932.

Reverse of the farewell card from the senior students shortly before our departure in the spring of 1932.

Shou Hsing Gung (Old Star Grandfather). God of immortality. His high forehead denotes wisdom. He leans on the Staff of Long Life, and holds the Peach of immortality in his left hand. (Photo taken by William Whitney Shrader in 2008).

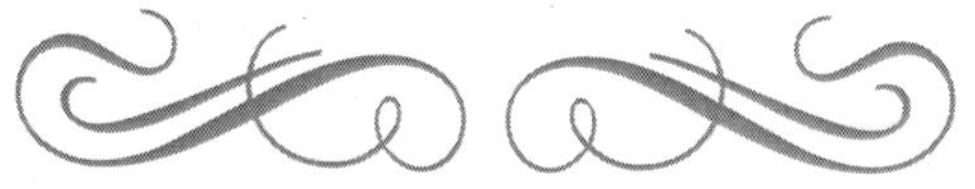

Baby and a Bamboo Chair

September 1928

Early morning fog, like puffs of dragon breath, moved across the mountain—*that Chinese dragon again!* I thought. The gray puffs blowing across the lawn settled in my stomach, stirring again the tormenting fears I had tried so hard to hide during our two years in this unpredictable land—the desperate China of 1928.

But it's not the baby coming so soon—it's going down into those Chinese streets, leaving my husband behind to close the cottage.

Glancing at the sturdy stone walls of our mountain cottage, the row of half-packed Chinese load baskets on the wide verandah, I thought, *Why did we ever come to China? Now when I need Ralph the most, must we be separated?* A small sense of guilt reminded me we had come to teach—to be friends with the people. But with the revolution smoldering about us what chance had there been?

I had hoped the baby would come in late August, in the cool security of our small mountain home. But Dr.

Dyer, flicking the pages of her calendar a week before had said, "Foochow is fairly quiet now. If the baby doesn't come by September third, you and I will go down to the city together. Vacation is over. I must open the hospital. Your husband can follow when he gets the cottage closed."

I was startled and started to speak, but the realistic eyes of the doctor and her crisp matter-of-fact voice allowed no dispute. I swallowed. She's not afraid. There's no need to worry.

She added, "We'll meet Monday at seven in front of the Three Bamboo Teahouse. We should be down the mountain by noon." Looking at her I could only think, she knows China. We'll be safe, me and my baby.

Each day I had taken long, uncomfortable walks. Now it was September third…the baby hadn't come.

Standing in front of the fog-bound cottage with Ralph and E-song, I saw the coolies emerge as from a Chinese painting, the chair swaying from two long bamboo shoulder poles. They eased the chair from their shoulders and bent over to place it on the lawn calling, "Hurry, Sinaniong. Hurry, Teacher's Wife. Great hurry this morning."

Why should they be in such a hurry today? I wondered, as Ralph urged me toward the chair.

I can't do this, Ralph—go down without you, I protested silently, remembering the mob-filled streets we had been through a year ago in the antiforeign riots of 1927.

Guessing my fear he put his hand on my shoulder—his eyes were not teasing now. He hesitated as he glanced toward the verandah and the round bamboo baskets waiting to be filled with household goods. "I could go down with you and then come right back."

I felt his hand tighten on my shoulder. Then through my mind flashed the picture of the long hot day, Ralph walking down the steep mountain, climbing back—the young men never rode. And I imagined his face—how tired after such a double trip.

"Oh, no, Ralph. Ridiculous!"

There was E-song. Glancing at his kindly face that seemed both old and young, I wanted to say, *couldn't E-song go with me?* But of course he couldn't. Ralph needed E-song to help close the cottage, board the windows, pack the baskets into forty-pound loads and manage the load carriers.

I saw relief replace the worry in Ralph's eyes as I lowered myself awkwardly into the chair. He handed me my white sun hat.

"It's the doctor you'll need. She'll be waiting for you at the Teahouse."

For a moment I felt better. The Three Bamboo Teahouse was only a ten-minute walk down our hill in the center of the small summer colony.

"Anyway, Ralph, please tell the men not to make waves."

We both knew the up-down, up-down sway of a chair could bring on labor. If only I had taken the chair ride a week ago!

The men were putting on their pointed straw hats and adjusting ragged towels over their calloused shoulders. Searching their bronzed faces for reassurance and observing their hard-muscled arms and legs, I thought two of them looked fit enough. Strong and good-natured. But the one they called Ibah, Old Uncle, wrinkled as a coconut shell—his legs were so thin. And the fourth was a mere boy.

Ralph spoke to the men in halting syllable-by-syllable Chinese. "Listen. You are not to make waves—swing the chair up and down. We've hired *four* men today, so no need to make waves." The men stared blankly at him. He called, "E-song, they can't understand me. Tell them not to make waves."

E-song strode over to the men, bearing his head proudly like a Mandarin, and rolled out a string of Chinese orders. *Good old E-song. He enjoys this. They won't make waves after that.*

I understood part of what he said, especially the repeated phrase, "*Moh coh laung*, don't make waves."

E-song reminded the men to stop for the doctor. The strong head-man at the front of the chair nodded and grinned.

"We understand. The Teacher's Wife is about to have a baby, to *iong giang*. We'll be ten-parts-whole careful." He turned to the men standing between the poles. "Remember, no waves."

"No waves," they promised. The creaking chair swayed as they adjusted the weight to their shoulders, the young fellow chuckling "*moh laung*." The men started.

I stretched out my hand, but all too soon the typhoon stone wall shut Ralph from sight. The thick mist wrapped me in a separate world. Let's go back…go back. Crooked pine trees appeared dimly in the mist and were sucked back into it. I felt so alone I shivered.

Straining to see a landmark, I told myself, *In a few minutes, I'll join the doctor*. This thought sustained me.

Presently the Chinese winds rising from the valley shifted the fog, and there were the glistening stones and tile roof of the Three Bamboos, silent, deserted. I couldn't see the doctor's sedan chair!

"Stop," I called to the men. "Wait for the doctor."

They lowered the chair. Old Uncle squinted into the mist. "Where is the doctor?"

"*Iseng-aaah*!" called the head man. "Doctor, *Iseng-aah*!" His voice was muffled and there was no answer.

We all listened, but there was only the drip, drip, drip, from an unseen terrace. The men squatted on their heels muttering. What were they saying? I tried to reach into the words, recognizing only a few, like friendly faces in a crowd. Doctor…hurry…angry… Oh, this language!

Without warning the men stood up raising the chair to their shoulders, and we were off. What were these men thinking of? I rapped on the poles to stop them.

"Wait. I must wait for the doctor!"

"The doctor will come," called the head man.

Again I rapped on the poles, but the men hurried on. The stone path became steps skirting terraces of sweet potato fields disappearing in fog. I thought of jumping from the chair, but that would be foolhardy.

Where was the doctor? Delayed by an emergency? Or perhaps she had gone ahead. Or was she close behind?

"She will come," Old Uncle reassured me. The Chinese had a way of knowing things. I had to believe them.

The men's quick feet fell into rhythm and the chair began to sway, up-down, up-down. *Never mind the waves*, I said to myself. But my heart pounded. What if the baby should be born on the way?

Rapping on the poles, I called, "No waves, no waves."

The men did not heed me. *Wrong tone*, I thought. The same word, spoken in different tones—high, low, rising, falling—had different meanings. I was probably saying, "No eggs."

I tried again, *moh laung*, in every one of the eight Foochow dialect tones. If only I could speak Chinese!

Suddenly Old Uncle jerked his head, shouting, "She says, 'don't make waves'," and looked back at me grinning.

"She says, 'no eggs'," called the young fellow. The men laughed. However, at a sharp command from Ibah, they broke the rhythm of their steps and the ride was smooth again. Back and forth over my head, they tossed their joke, "No waves, no eggs." And for a minute, I laughed with them.

Yet despite the smooth ride, I could sense an urgency. *Why, why did they run with me?*

The path became steep, down a fog-filled ravine, past floating bamboo groves. Now it widened on a ledge where a crude stone teahouse stood. Surely they would stop here. But no, we passed it like a panting dragon and down again. A gust of wind blew up from the valley breaking the mist into shreds, and we were below the cloud.

Now I looked into a sheer gorge so close by the trail that I clutched the chair arms. *Heaven help us*, I begged, hoping that the men's feet would be as sure as those of mountain goats. Below I could see the steps curving steeply down, at times following the very edge of the precipice—down to the hot plains. And in the distance the Min River, a winding silver thread. Far ahead the tile roofs of the city shimmered—hours away. And that dark point against the skyline, was it the White Pagoda? Yes, the White Pagoda that marked our home, and the hospital and the college where we taught. Would we ever make it?

Down we went—swaying around the curves. I held fast to the chair arms watching the men's feet slapping the stones faster than a swiftly turning wheel. What if the lead man should stumble and pitch the chair forward—the gorge right below us? *Don't look*, I thought, closing my eyes. But I had to look, and every muscle braced.

Then I remembered. "Go backwards—I want to ride backwards!" The men paid no attention. I called the word aloud in all the Chinese tones. Again Ibah jerked his head toward me.

"Slow down. She wants to ride backwards!"

The men grunted to a halt, put the chair down, Ibah grinning broadly, then on the narrow path reversed the chair. As it swung around, I could see the bottom of the gorge so far below—but so close…

Now I rode leaning back. *Watch those white clouds*, I told myself. *This is really fun. I'll bet none of my friends at home ever had a ride like this to have a baby!* But my eyes sought the trail above. There was no sign of the doctor.

Relax, I told myself. The baby stirred within me. I felt the pressure of a foot, or was it an arm? It pushed hard against my side, and gently I pushed it back. *Don't get in a hurry*, I said. *Please take it easy. We'll make it. For you, we'll make it.*

As the chair swayed and the poles creaked, I remembered another teahouse near the foot of the mountain and looked at my watch. We'd been gone an hour. How long for a first child? How long to the city? Perhaps I should stop at the teahouse to wait for the doctor? No, don't panic. What if the baby should arrive in a hut blackened by charcoal fires with only an old wife to help? *Dear God*, I begged, *if You want this child to be born in what I consider a normal manner, it's up to You!*

I tried to sleep, but frightening memories slid through my mind—the crowded streets, the soldiers breaking through the compound gate, cries of *Dong-pay*, *Huang-guay*, long-nose foreigners! The ugly posters on the street—those distorted cartoon faces of white men. The terror of that day—seeing ourselves as others see us!

Of course there had to be a revolution. I recalled sights of misery—the bandit-ridden people of the countryside—hungry hollow-eyed, hopeless. It's been a long time coming. We believe in it, too. Why can't they know we believe in it? Must there always be a barrier between us? If only it could be a friendly revolution!

If only E-song were here. He could talk to the people, help me through those streets. Don't think—try to sleep. It's quiet now in the city, they say. I closed my eyes, forcing out the ugly pictures, and for a while was riding through clean streets of an American city in our old Chevy, and Ralph was at the wheel.

We stopped briefly at the stone hut called Foot of the Mountain Teahouse. The doctor was nowhere in sight.

Another ten minutes and the mountain trail ended abruptly on the plain, becoming a narrow path that zigzagged through flat rice paddies. The men's sandals slapped the stones in sing-song rhythm. The dizzying sun pressed down, and the creaking poles swayed the chair, up-down, up-down, in time to the men's quick steps. I braced against the sway of the heaviness within me.

"*Moh laung*, no waves!" I called.

The men laughed and mimicked me good-naturedly. "No waves, no waves—no eggs, no eggs!"

Again the ride was smooth and the men eased the burden on their shoulders with their chant. *Ai-ha*, *ai-ha*, *ai-ha*, I chanted silently with them. And a century went by, or so the next half hour seemed.

Now spreading its shade across the path and dropping great roots to the ground, I saw the ancient banyan tree protecting its little village. Scrawny chickens slept dustily between twisted roots. Nothing stirred in the heat of the cobbled court leading over to a small mud-and-tile teahouse.

"Oh, no, not again!" I groaned as the men lowered the chair, tossed off their hats, wiped their faces and strode across the court to drink tea. No use waiting for the doctor here. My muscles ached. I wanted to get home. But the men needed their tea. It was the custom!

Perhaps I, too, should go for tea. But this was not a public teahouse for foreigners. It was not the custom.

An old woman in a short blue coat and patched trousers spied the chair and stumped across the rough stones on her stiff bound feet. She leaned over me and her dim eyes peered curiously, then wrinkled into pleased surprise.

"*Ai*! *Dong-pay*, a long-nose. And she's soon to have a baby!"

I shrank back from her old hands clutching the chair arm and smiled up at her with effort. "I'm a Sinaniong, a Teacher's Wife."

Old Mother, beckoning palms down, shrilled to the courtyard, "Come see. A foreign woman. And she's about to have a child."

Several peasant women trailed by children moved toward us waking the chickens into a squawking flurry. Forcing a smile I called the familiar greeting exchanged for courtesy in that part of China, "Peace—peace."

Old Mother grinned at me. "Peace—peace. Have you eaten your rice?" I recognized this greeting also.

"Who is it?" a broad-faced woman called.

"*Dong-pay*, a long-nose," said Old Mother. "She speaks our tongue."

"*Dong-pay*, peace—peace!" the broad-faced woman said.

The field-browned peasants surrounded me, their short jackets clinging to their wet bodies, trousers rolled to their sturdy thighs, dusty bare feet unbound. A star of white jasmine blossomed in the coil of a woman's black hair. One girl, her short coat covering her swollen body, advanced cautiously and peered over Old Mother's shoulder. A copper-naked small boy, seeing my white face, started to whimper. *He's afraid of me*, I thought with sudden surprise.

"No fear, no fear," comforted his mother as I reached out to him, but he buried his face against her legs sobbing.

They crowded close. "Ai, the Sinaniong is about to have a baby. When? Today?

I tried to smile. My Chinese words faltered. "Not yet, oh, not yet."

"But soon," Broad-Face asserted. "I can tell."

"Her ankles are not swollen," pointed out Old Mother with her knobby fingers.

"That is true." They nodded after careful inspection.

"That does not have to be," said Broad-Face.

"Oh, yes, it did with me," argued Jasmine Flower. "Is this your first?" I nodded.

"Boy or girl?" asked the pregnant girl shyly.

"How can you ask such a thing?" The child's mother poked a finger at the girl's full coat. "Of course, a son first."

One reached out and felt the cloth of my light cotton dress, another pointed to my shoes. *They're just curious*; I comforted myself, listening carefully as their questions came fast.

"Where is your husband? Where do you go now?"

I pointed to the city. "To the foreigners' hill by the White Pagoda."

"*Ai-ha*, many fields from here. And the city to go through." Old Mother counted on her fingers. "One… two…three hours from here."

"Yes. Please tell the chair men to hurry."

Old Mother considered this while the others watched her, then she turned and stumped back across the court to the teahouse. The women continued their questions. I answered, groping for words that they repeated, laughing and correcting my tones. Soon Old Mother returned, balancing across the rough stones, and held out to me a cup of tea with both hands.

"Tea, Sinaniong. Drink it. It will give you strength."

I thought, *Typhoid, cholera, dysentery—but how can I refuse?* And I was desperately thirsty.

"Drink it, drink the tea. And the coolies will come."

I sipped the tea. It was very hot, it would be safe. I smiled at the Old Woman. Then recalling that village people often do not have even a leaf of tea to put in their own tea water, I fumbled in my coin bag for a few copper coins.

Broad-Face was saying, "Yes, tea is strength." Turning to the others, she pointed to me. "This foreign woman is going to have a child, the same as we do. They are born across the sea and have strange faces and pale eyes. But they are made like us—all the same way."

The women stared at me, and their eyes widened with slow wonder. They nodded. "That is true, *si-sik*, true. Made like us!" At this thought they laughed, looking sidelong at each other. "Made like us!"

Old Mother shook her wrinkled face at them. "Of course, you stupids. What did you think?"

The chair men were coming as I held out my coin-filled hand to Old Mother. She waved it off.

"No, no. Please no. This is but a small gift from one mother to another."

"A small gift," the others urged, eagerly and without laughter now. "A small gift, one mother to another!"

The head man lifted the chair. "Let's go."

"Hurry," said Old Mother. "The Teacher's Wife is about to *iong giang*. Don't stop for tea again. Take her straight to the foreign place by the White Pagoda."

A boy, a girl, I thought, waving back, if only I get there. The way across the fields was just as hot, but something had changed.

After an hour the path between the rice fields widened to a road lined with food shops, and people lustily buying and selling. As we approached the city wall and the arch of East Gate, I felt my hands grow tight on the chair again, remembering that inside the city we would pass an abandoned temple where soldiers were always quartered. It was the soldiers who, indoctrinated by the radicals, put up the ugly posters and aroused the people to attack the foreigners. I tried to swallow the tightness in my throat.

"Out of the way!" my head man shouted. A blind beggar was tapping his way directly in front of us. Here, under the broad city gate was the thieves' market, and a crowd of beggars squatting in the shade, extending their claw hands and leprous sores and wailing their chant, "Give a little; win merit; give a little." A ragged woman got up and ran along by my chair, a baby clutching at her sagging breast. I felt my eyes sting with a sudden anger that such things could be, and dropped some copper coins into her extended hand. *What use?* I thought. *There is so little we can do, so very little.*

We moved from the cool arch of the gate into the pushing crowds of the narrow street. I hoped that angry hands would not claim me. *But look*, I thought, *they don't notice me. No one even looks at me! Why should they? Look at that crowd around the street vendor.* I sniffed the garlic-seasoned pork balls wrapped in dumplings bubbling in his open kettle and watched the people pushing around a food stall, too busy bargaining for bunches of leeks and mustard greens or slippery, smelly fish to notice the foreign woman in the sedan chair.

There was a smell of bucket-carried sewage. And a moment later the whiff of dried herbs. It all made me sick. *Hurry, get me out of here*, I thought. My chair men, with jerking halts to avoid load bearers, grunted their refrain, "Make way, make way."

At the end of this street the neglected temple stood, the temple used by soldiers. Would they see me now and start the cry, "foreign devil" again?

We passed the last of the rattan shops. Now, here it is. The dirty stone-paved courtyard of the temple. Soldiers? Yes, a few, but lounging idly, they paid me only an indifferent glance.

As relief flooded through me, I closed my eyes. A few minutes later, I was jolted to a sudden stop as the chair men halted in a tangle of traffic. A large load-bearer carrying two heavy baskets looked impassively, then stared, right into my face. Pointing his chin at me, he shouted to the street, "Look, look! A foreign woman, a long-nose!"

Quickly I encircled my arms about my unborn baby. "No! No!"

"Make way," called my head chair man impatiently.

For a second I felt numb. So it was coming. They would attack me! Then, involuntarily, I leaned forward and, looking straight into the coolie's eyes, called, "*Bing-ang*, peace, peace! Have you eaten your rice?"

The coolie with unpredictable swiftness changed expression. His eyes, meeting mine, wrinkled into a smile, his broad mouth grinned. "You speak our tongue! Where do you go?"

I recognized that friendly greeting of the road, *Where do you go*? As the chair men moved ahead, I called over my shoulder, "To Peace Street."

"Oh, to Peace Street, under the White Pagoda. Travel well!"

I took off my sun hat, wiped my face with the skirt of my cotton dress, and my trembling gradually stopped. I thought, *Why, these people are friendly, if they're not made to hate.* And the idea flowed through my whole body, comforting every tense muscle. Through the long stretch of South Street, almost the length of the city, I dozed.

At last, Peace Street, deserted in the noon heat. Ahead I could see our compound wall, its wooden gate closed. And down a short street to the right the Mission Hospital with the blue Chinese characters above its door, its wall-gate closed also. In the background the White Pagoda rose spreading its peace.

We stopped before the compound gate. The head chair man knocked. "Open, open, Ibah, open!" A small window in the gate slid back and an old man peered through, squinting his rheumy eyes into the glare of the street.

Head man said, "The Teacher's Wife has come. Open, you lazy son-of-a-turtle. Hurry. She is about to *iong giang.*"

Ibah struggled with the iron bar. "But there is no one here. And I was given orders not to let anyone enter." He swung the gate half-open but blocked the way, looking at me cautiously. "The doctor has not come back and not even a nurse is here."

Oh, I thought, *no doctor! And is he going to stop me?* "Please, Ibah."

Head man pushed his foot against the gate. The doors creaked wide as the men brushed past the blinking gatekeeper and moved up the steps onto the lawns surrounding the six empty homes of our compound. At the top of the hill, I glimpsed a brick cottage, Ralph's and mine, still closed and barred fast.

At its door I climbed out of the chair and paid the men their wages. They wiped their shoulders with the ragged towels and held out pleading hands to me. "Extra coppers, extra coppers for tea money. Truly-truly, Sinaniong, we made no waves."

"*Moh laung*, no eggs." The boy grinned, laughing at his joke so that the head man gave him a shove. I gave them coppers.

Smiling, they picked up the chair, so light now, and thanked me. "The doctor will come, no fear. And may it be a beautiful boy!"

I was alone in the empty silence with the empty brick houses, their windows shuttered. Palms drooped above the uncut grass. I listened. Only a mynah bird called a shrill mocking welcome. Street noises drifted up from that other world below our hill.

A step sounded and I turned. Oh, joy, the doctor's cook who had been caretaking during her vacation. He invited me into her open home adjoining our own and prepared a bowl of noodles on the charcoal stove, chatting reassuringly.

"No fear, Sinaniong, she will come. This doctor is a woman of will. When she says a thing, she means it."

I watched the sun set red behind the distant mountains, and the evening skies wrap the White Pagoda in gold. For ten centuries this pagoda had looked down on scenes of birth and death, and the city had multiplied about its feet. I thought, *Birth can…birth does take place without…*

From the bed on the doctor's screened verandah, I could watch the pagoda. I tried to sleep. Quiet now, no fear, the doctor will come. Sleep. But my ears strained for voices, and the stars behind the pagoda wheeled slowly across the sky. Muscles ached. *This means nothing. Draw a curtain against fear.*

Night edged, edged into day. The pagoda's night whiteness sharpened, turned pink, then glowed, reflecting the eastern sky's red streaks. Ah! It was the color of pain! Quickly, dress. And please, may there be one nurse returned from vacation at the hospital.

As I hurried down the hill toward the compound gate, someone was coming up the walk toward me swinging two baskets from his pole.

"E-song, oh, E-song! What are you doing here so early?"

"No trouble, Sinaniong." He slid his heavy baskets to the ground. "The Sinang, your husband, is delayed because of a load-carrier's strike. But I bring you his letter and some things you might need. Come, I'll open your house."

"No, I go to the hospital."

"Already? But, you haven't eaten rice."

"Can I help that?"

His eyes looked straight into mine with an ageless wisdom, and suddenly I saw him no longer the servant, but a man of dignity, who with his heavy load has risked that mountain by night. "Have no fear," he said sternly, and the strength in his eyes gave strength to my shaking knees.

He picked up his loads and turned toward the gate. "Come then to the hospital. The doctor has come."

"The doctor? She's here?"

Stepping lightly ahead of me, he looked back with a smile that crinkled his whole bronze face. "And may it be a beautiful boy!"

Already in front of the hospital returning patients were gathering. In the hall I found the doctor briskly instructing two black-braided girls whose fingers were fumbling the cloth buttons of their Chinese blue uniforms. Glancing at my face, she said, "Hurry, here is the Sinaniong. Get the room ready."

To me she said, "You were lucky. You got away because your chair men hurried you off unnoticed in the fog. The strike—you know. I tried all day to get my men to bring me down, but none dared work till it was settled."

"Oh, the strike. That's why they ran with me!" And I thought, *That fog, it must have been a good dragon after all!*

The doctor continued, "It's the revolution. They said they would be beaten if they did. But when your men returned after dark they slipped in to me and said, 'The Sinaniong needs you. Hurry, we carry you down.' A double trip and a double risk! But would I come?"

"Oh, that mountain in the dark!"

"I had a flashlight," said the doctor, and pushed me toward the stairs to the delivery room.

Several hours later, when I was in my room, eyes resting happily on the crib in the corner, the two nurses came shyly to me. One held out a blue covered bowl.

"Chicken soup. We made it especially for you, with special Chinese herbs. If you drink the broth of a chicken made this way, it will help a woman recover her strength and have milk for her baby. Our custom, Sinaniong, drink it."

Such broth! *A good custom*, I thought. The girls stood close by watching till I finished it.

Then they tiptoed to the crib and drew the mosquito net aside. "*Ai-ha*, the little girl child is ten-parts-whole good to look at. Rest your heart, Sinaniong, next time a boy!"

I groped drowsily for words. "*Si-sik*, truly, my heart rests. She is what I wanted." But where was the vocabulary in Chinese or any language to explain that she was what I really wanted for the first child, all along the way?

And something else. Something the baby had brought me quite unexpectedly. Something about a bamboo chair and a cup of tea, a mountain trail by night, and some other things—or was it *people*? Ralph, hurry!

But I don't have to explain, I thought. Listen… One of the nurses was leaning over the crib singing a Chinese nursery rhyme:

Green-gold bird eats the paupaus.

Next-door child sings a song.

It is not his parents who teach him the song.

It is the strange bird…

And from their hearts together

Comes the song.

I said, "Teach me the song."
And she taught me, line by line.

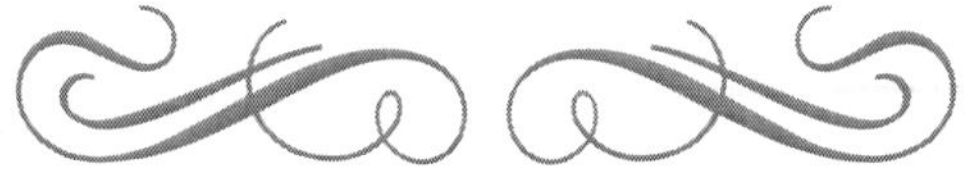

Precious Jade

Fall 1928

The morning I returned from the hospital, E-song carried the baby in a two-handled bamboo basket. He strode ahead of me, his short stocky frame erect with a solemnity that made him seem tall, and he held the basket out in front of him as if he were bearing a royal princess. We were a triumphal procession. He brushed aside the children in Peace Street who tried to peak into the basket, "Shoo…get back," and barked a sharp order to Ibah at the compound gate to open quickly. When we reached the front porch of our home at the top of the hill, he set the basket down and leaning over had his first real look at the small face staring up at him, at the tiny waving fists.

"Look," he said to me in Chinese. "Look…a girl…but look at her, Sinaniong!" Beyond that he was speechless as his solemn face lighted in the most radiant smile.

You would think he was her father, I thought, laughing to myself. My heart warmed at his loyalty.

While in the hospital, I had advertised for an amah to take care of the new baby, but not a single nursemaid had applied. Because of the antiforeign propaganda, of course, no one dared to come.

I was really in despair. So soon after my arrival home, I was surprised to discover, standing in my front hall, a young Chinese woman in neat black jacket and trousers. She said, "I'm an amah." I could have hugged her!

"Tell me about yourself."

"My name is Ai-nuk" (Precious Jade)

Her thin face closed. She was silent. Then she blurted out, "I'm a widow. I have to work." After a long pause, she slung the words at me, "When our child was four years old, my husband was killed in an antiforeign riot."

Her anger struck me like the stones of the rioters. I winced. Too late I added, "I'm sorry."

The amah said abruptly, "Where is your child?"

Leading her to the pram on the screened porch I had thought, this woman is "eating bitterness"...and she is so small. Can she possibly carry the heavy cans of water and do the hard scrubbing for the baby? And has she any love to spare?

Lifting the mosquito net, Ai-nuk looked down at the baby and said in Chinese, "It's too hot for her here... what's her name?"

"Katharine...she's three weeks old."

Ai-nuk tried to repeat the unfamiliar syllables. "Ka-trine...Ka-trine," and glanced up at me.

I nodded, smiling. "Well...yes...Ka-trine."

She leaned over and gently stroking the baby's wet forehead her face lighted. "Ka-trine...this is Ai-nuk. Do you understand? Ai-nuk."

Seeing this gesture and the wistfulness in her face, I thought, she has love...at least for the baby.

Caressing the child again, she murmured, "My little one was like this...all the same...only now not so small."

I thought the amah was going to smile. Here was one who liked babies. I was desperate...I would take the chance. "You will be amah for us?"

"I will be amah for Ka-trine. I'll go for my things and be back tomorrow." She did not return my smile.

Watching her walk away—so small and straight—or was it defiant—I felt both relief and misgiving.

I need not have worried about her work. She carried the baby wash-water and scrubbed the small clothes till I marveled that anything remained. Then she wheeled Ka-trine under the banyan tree, and later as the child walked, they played together in a small pavilion in its shade.

Sometimes I joined them there fascinated as I watched her teaching Ka-trine her first Chinese words. But when we were alone—always when she talked with me—her eyes would cloud like the smoldering charcoal embers on our stove, and she would let me know in quiet bitter tones that I was a foreigner—I was every foreigner.

I understood this bitterness she held between us. Someday, I determined, I will be able to do something for her to prove we aren't all Imperialists.

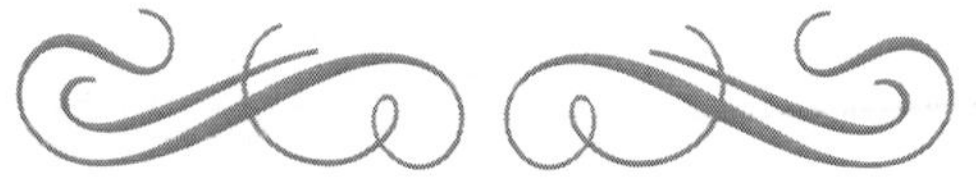

E-song and the Law

Fall 1928

Our family revolved around two hubs—Huo-seng and E-song. If anything happened to either hub we knew our household would collapse!

Huo-seng was *Cio-dio*, Lord of the Kitchen, of that there was no doubt. He did not welcome my presence in his smoked red tile cubicle with its large red tile stove arrayed with steaming water cans blackened by years of charcoal smoke. Scholarly Huo-seng with his major-domo bearing, gray hair, and penetrating Asian eyes that scarcely concealed their amusement at me, was entirely competent here. He was necessary to us, and he knew this; he was able to keep me in my place!

Without him there would be no boiled water safe to drink and no Chinese vegetables and odd hunks of meat he had bargained over in the markets and which appeared on our table after ordeal-by-fire on that unmentionable stove. Without Huo-seng we and our constant guests would go hungry. He suggested and planned and produced, and I was glad that it was so, and did not dare cross him!

E-song was different. Without E-song there would be no clean clothes scrubbed on a hand-made wood washboard in warm suds. Without him there would be no cans of hot bath water to baste ourselves in, because there would be no charcoal fires, and more important, no water. Standard Oil tins swaying from his shoulder pole, E-song carried all the water for our household up the hill from the compound well. He mopped our floors and shook our three large rugs. He did this heavy work with a quiet easy grace. Though rated as a coolie—(*ku-li*, meaning "bitter labor") he had become to us a "gentleman"—a friend—almost a member of our family.

Upon Huo-seng and E-song our existence depended. Moreover, they were the friendly bridge between our small island of whiteness and the oriental world smoldering like a volcano around us.

Around these two hubs, the wheels of our home had rolled smoothly the two years we had been in China. But now I had a presentiment this good fortune could not last. From Canton had come rumors that foreigners, driven to despair because of servant problems, were leaving the country.

Despite rumors, I spent the hour after my return from the hospital in a state of bliss settling Ka-trine in her new domain with E-song's eager help. Then Huo-seng, back from the street, knocked at my door. I assumed it was to take accounts. It was.

First he admired the baby, making no mention of the fact that she was only a girl, and with a formal bow, placed in her crib a bright red lacquer rice bowl and matching chopsticks. Then after a prolonged session with an abacus, Chinese pen, and confusing monetary problems, he cleared his throat and said, "*Hia-huoi.*"

My heart sank for that meant, "This and that." Sometimes it meant trouble.

"Sinaniong, it has been my unworthy pleasure to work for you for two years. Now I must leave your honorable household. I eat bitterness to tell you this."

My world swayed. I felt the earth opening beneath me. When I could find the words, I cried, "Oh no, Huo-seng. You can't go. I will eat bitterness too, if you leave us."

He was firm. "My wife is ill. Back at our village my family needs me. I must go."

"You'll return as soon as you can?"

He shook his head. "The Sinaniong will be able to find another cook." I wanted to cry.

He left the next day after filling the drinking water jars, making an extra bowl of white butter from the buffalo cow milk, baking several loaves of potato yeast bread, and stewing an appalling amount of the tough local beef.

I panicked and tried to figure out the real reason for his leaving. Had he felt we had not allowed him to make enough squeeze—the more or less legitimate percentage he kept from every egg, vegetable, and basket of charcoal? In this way cooks were allowed to supplement the pitifully small wages prescribed by the social order. Or had he "lost face" in an incident that had occurred while I was at the hospital?

One Sunday morning Ralph had met him, by chance, in the hall carrying a plate of waffles downstairs to his ailing wife. This had broken two laws of our compound, which we had felt too harsh. The servants were not supposed to have their families "live in" with us in our homes. To compensate they took time off. Grandmothers died with an unbelievable frequency. Special-day festivals must be observed with the families. However, when Huo-seng moved his wife in with him for a week to their downstairs quarters with their own kitchen, we pretended not to notice.

The other rule was that the Chinese could not use our food supplies. They prepared and ate their own rice and spicy smelling tidbits in their kitchen entirely separate from ours. It seemed no crime to Ralph that Huo-seng should take a plate of waffles down to his wife—we often shared some specialty. And both he and Huo-seng appeared to notice nothing. If Huo-seng had felt he had lost face, that could be serious. But it seemed too minor an incident to sever our happy relationship.

More likely, we guessed, he was under pressure from the labor unions, newly organized by the Nationalists. Now the unions appeared to be taking over the government, especially harassing foreigners by creating servant problems, using this as an antiforeign weapon…a good way for the left wing revolutionaries to get even with the white man for a century or two of exploitation.

We asked our teacher, Iong Sinang, when he came the next day why Huo-seng had left, but he either pretended to be, or was completely ignorant of the cause. He did write a very Chinese-proper letter to our cook asking him to return. When he had finished brushing the black characters on the rice paper, he read the literary phrases to me with pride. It sounded impressive, and I was sure it would bring Huo-seng back, either with or without his wife.

Two days later a letter came from Huo-seng, which Iong Sinang read to me. "Though my heart can be in two places at once, unfortunately my body cannot. I must remain in my village where my family needs me."

I was in despair. I had struggled with, and been completed defeated by, the charcoal monster in the kitchen, which only smoked as I fanned it, causing my eyes to stream, while the baby screamed and the typhoid-dysentery laden water would not boil. E-song, with pleased alacrity, had taken over the marketing. Then noticing my distress, he also built the fire, boiled the drinking water, made our bread, and assumed more of the cooking chores while he continued to carry the water up the hill, buckets deftly swinging from his pole. This doubling on rigidly stratified duties was breaking a custom. But he did it with a sweetness of spirit that cemented our feelings for him. We were not blind to a certain motive in all this.

After the disappointing letter from Huo-seng arrived, E-song said, "*Hia-huoi*, Sinaniong. If the Sinang and you would like it, I will be your cook and find a 'boy' to do the coolie work."

I was overjoyed. That E-song had little training as a cook seemed unimportant. Then I hesitated. "But do you have a union card permitting you?"

He said, "I think I can arrange it."

Busy with my new responsibilities in the nursery, and training Ai-nuk to help with the baby so that I could teach at the college and continue language study, I let E-song take over completely as Lord of the Kitchen. He grew two inches taller and more solemn. The food was bleak at times—the cakes solid, the vegetables watery, the meat boiled to shoe leather. But the bread was excellent, he was willing to learn, and we were at peace. No boy appeared, but E-song assured me he was looking for the right one. And now when he walked down the hill in his starched blue long-coat with his market basket in his hand, his thin face wore a look of pure pleasure.

Thus our family managed for several weeks with its single hub, E-song. The fragile Ai-nuk gave us loyal support except when she felt it necessary to complain loudly that she had insufficient hot water. She was content for hours pushing Ka-trine in her old English "pram" under the banyan tree, cooing Chinese to her or jabbering with the other amahs. Life, I thought, was moving with serenity too good to last.

Then it happened. I was startled one morning by a sound of great shouting—of agonized terror. From the dining room window, I saw a group of struggling men moving from the rear toward the front of the house. I raced to the porch, hearing the angry shouts, "*Moh… moh!*—No, no!" and I thought, that is E-song's voice!

On the lawn I saw three strong men grappling with E-song who was struggling to free himself. His long white kitchen apron was looped about his neck and being pulled by one of the men so that the neck-string was strangling him. I heard him retching and saw him turning white.

I thought, *They are killing him!* And cried wildly, "*Moh, moh!* Help, somebody help!"

Dr. Dyer's cook and houseboy came running out, but when they saw what was happening, they stood helplessly back, wide-eyed.

I cried, "Run to the college. Call Choi Sinang (Ralph), Leger Teacher, anyone!"

The cook shot through the wall gate. Never had I seen any cook move so fast.

The struggle continued. E-song, strangling and retching, was losing strength. The men jerked him along the walk, jerk by hard jerk, toward the front gate. I followed crying helplessly, "*Moh! Moh!*"

At last I saw Ralph and Mr. Leger coming on the run. I heard Mr. Leger's command to Ralph, "Go to the police station!" Ralph's breathless, "Where?" and the reply, "Out the gate, and to your right a block. Hurry!"

Ralph ran past the struggling group, leaped down the steps, and disappeared. I followed him in my mind as he put his football training to the test up the narrow street. "Hurry, Ralph, hurry!" I cried after him.

Several Chinese had appeared and placed themselves between the thugs and the gate, slowing their progress. Mr. Leger shouted to the intruders, "Stop! Let go!" Looking from E-song to Mr. Leger, the slightly built scholar, lashing them with a torrent of angry Chinese, they loosened their hold. E-song took this chance to snatch the string from his neck. I breathed again with him.

Something in the authority of Mr. Leger's voice intimidated the thugs, but only for a second. One of them spat out, "*Huang gwei*—Foreign Devil," and I was afraid they would attack him. Instead they began shaking and pummeling E-song again. Mr. Leger stood straight and close to them. He commanded, "Out! Get out!" The men began pulling E-song to the gate. In the intervening second, however, he had slipped the apron from his neck and flung it away. I saw a servant grab it up.

The bewildered gateman standing at the foot of the steps to the gatehouse had barred the gate. Mr. Leger called to him, "Watch for the police. Open when they come." The old man nodded.

It all depended on timing now. If the thugs got E-song into the street, he would be gone from what small protection we could offer. My knees shook. I thought, *Won't Ralph ever come? Will the police come at all?*

Mr. Leger ran past the struggling men to put himself between them and the gate. At that moment Ralph and three red-faced puffing policemen pushed open the double-gate doors and raced up the steps blocking the way of the thugs.

I felt like cheering but saw it was too soon—the thugs were bigger than the police. However, one of the police waved a revolver and the men let go their hold. I could not understand the quick, angry words. At last the policeman with the gun shouted an order, and the thugs drew back from E-song. Then E-song, Ralph, and Mr. Leger, all flanked by the police, marched down the steps, out the gate in the direction of the police station.

I went back to my house, knees like rubber, threw myself across the bed, and cried. Presently I heard a gentle cough and rolled over. It was Ai-nuk. Her slight body was trembling.

Ai-yah, Sinaniong. Trouble...always trouble! And now what will we do? There is only a little water in my jar for the baby's washing. And not a drop of boiled water on the kitchen stove for drinking. What will we do?"

From the nursery I heard a wail. The Chinese phrase that had so often irritated me came to my lips, "There is no help for it." Unwittingly I stood up. I had work to do.

It seemed hours—hours of fanning a smoking charcoal fire that would not burn...hours of apprehension—till I heard Ralph returning, I supposed with E-song. He came in alone.

"What happened?" I asked as casually as I could.

He sat down weakly. "They arrested E-song...there will be a hearing later, in a few days..."

"E-song?" I cried.

"They said it was for E-song's protection..."

"And the thugs?"

"Oh—they let the thugs go!"

I sat down as the world spun around me and the tears ran down my cheeks, and Ralph tried, futilely, to comfort me. Thus we were left without our two hubs—without Huo-seng and E-song…without water or fire, or any appreciable amount of food. Worst of all, we were left without our bridge to that other strange world about us.

Days later Mr. Leger told us that E-song had been freed but was under advice to work in a different part of the city. For more than a week, we struggled grimly through the maze of unaccustomed chores. Then one morning I discovered E-song at work in the kitchen as if he had never been away. I could barely refrain from throwing my arms around his neck.

"E-song…oh, E-song!" I cried.

Now, *hia houi*, he told me, he would work as "boy" again, and he had heard the labor union was sending us a cook!

Heaven was partially restored…and it was due to these events that we made a great discovery…we discovered Ding-Chung…

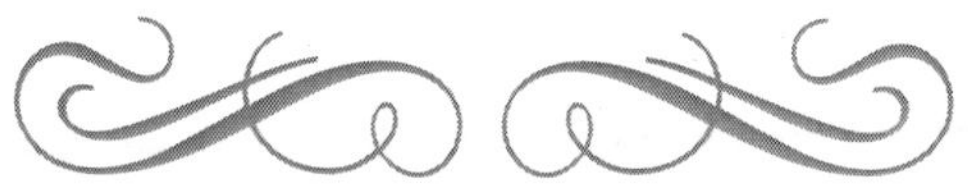

Ding-chung—Magic Worker

Fall 1928

So I return to the day that the water jars were empty, and E-song in jail…that was what led to our discovery of Ding-chung.

That was why, the same evening, as the dinner hour approached, Ralph was in the college courtyard on the bottom of the stone steps which wound up to our compound, with a precariously balanced shoulder-pole over his shoulder and two Standard Oil tins three-fourths full of water he had just drawn from the college well. Gathered about watching him were a group of students in their long blue coats. I was watching also from the wall-gate at the top of the steps. This was going to be worth watching.

The students laughed good naturedly, pointing at Ralph, "Choi Sinang—Shrader, Teacher—*co kulik*—makes like a coolie!" He attempted to turn and wave at them, but his hands were occupied. As he bent, adjusting and lifting the weight, they repeated, "Choi Sinang *co kulik*!" Ralph moved, with effort, up a step, and they clapped, laughing aloud, "*Co kulik, co kulik*!"

With the next few steps, the tins began to sway and water slopped over Ralph's legs, dousing his trousers. He stopped for better balance. The students, watching him closely, laughed and clapped. Ralph looked back, grinning at them. I could see he was red and perspiring. Obviously this was turning into more of a project than he had anticipated when earlier he had assured me, "Don't worry. I can carry a few loads of water till we get someone."

He continued, slow step by slow straining step. The buckets swayed. The water sloshed. I knew he would never give in—"face" now demanded that he carry through. Partly I knew he was trying to set the students an example. Chinese scholars *never* demeaned themselves doing physical labor. They still prided themselves on growing a long fingernail now and then—that ancient symbol of status. Physically they were undeveloped, prone to tuberculosis.

So, Ralph reasoned, if by demonstrating that he, the foreign teacher, was not above carrying water in an emergency, it would be a useful lesson to the students.

The splotches of water up the steps were evidence that this was a skill he had not mastered. By the time he was halfway up and breathless, and the students still watching every move, a large part of the water had slopped from the tins making the load easier. Finally, puffing and a trifle grim, he reached the top. The students applauded.

"That's enough," I said. "Put it in the big red jar by the kitchen. We won't wash tomorrow."

But he was in one of his determined moods. "I'm just getting the hang of it. And I've got to show them I can do it." As he said this, balancing his shoulder pole, he pointed with his chin to the students below.

I laughed. "Exactly like the Chinese, the way you pointed your chin!"

He said grimly, "Well, how else can you point when your hands are busy? Get out of the way." And he moved toward the back balustrade where three huge and empty water jars stood.

In a moment he went back down the steps and filled his tins, not so full this time, with a second load. He joked with the students, who, as he made his second trip up, watched him now with a new quietness. Nothing was said. I saw that the water did not slop so much. He seemed to be getting his stride. He went back for a third load. I knew it took five or six loads to fill even one jar. I went into the house.

He told me later that when he reached the well this time, a student stepped forward from the group and said, "Sinang, I am a boy who lived in the country before I came to this school. I am not very skillful with carrying pole, but I have experience. If Choi Teacher will let me, I will be glad to carry a load of water up the hill for him."

Ralph made a polite protest, but the student quickly rolled up his wide trousers, filled the tins from the well bucket, lifted the load, and moved smoothly up the steps.

Though he had filled the buckets, he did not spill a drop. The crowd, which had grown, remained quiet. Ralph heard someone ask, "Who is it?" And another answer, "Ding-chung. It's Ding-chung!"

How much this might cost Ding-chung in the loss of "face" before the other students, we could only speculate. We were sure it must have taken real courage. I asked Ralph more about Ding-chung.

He said, "You remember the show they put on recently? He was the magician—who did the slight-of-hand tricks."

I said, "Oh, the clown—the one who played the foolish coolie in the skit."

"He's the one. I judge he's one of the most liked boys in the college. It's almost a phenomenon. He's from the country, not from a family of officials or scholars or administrators like most of them. But he seems to be quite a leader. This may make an impression!"

The incident reached the principal's ears. It was then that Ralph learned about Ding-chung's special problem.

Robert told Ralph, "The boy's in a difficult spot. The bandits have been busy around their village. He asked recently if I knew any way he could work for his room and board, which is almost unknown here among students. He's very bright. I told him we could give him a tuition scholarship if he could manage the rest. Board is now four dollars a month—little enough. But when you realize it is probably more than his father gets a month… well, and there are other expenses."

Ralph thought a moment, then asked, "Do you think he would consider doing some work late afternoons in our garden? That would mean carrying water and caring for the small vegetable garden and a few flowers and lawn."

Robert considered. "It would be breaking all precedent—a very healthy thing. I'll ask him."

The next day Ding-chung moved into the tiny room on the ground level by the garden. He brought with him his bed quilt, a small bundle of clothes, his straw farmer hat he had used in the show, his books, his bamboo flute, and his gay disposition.

Ding-chung added much to our household. As a gardener he did quite well. In the hour or two a day which he gave to our garden, in place of basketball and the physical education course, his quick fingers worked more magic than the full-time loafing of the worthless man the labor-union had wished upon us and whom Ralph had finally decided must leave or die. He left. We suddenly wondered, could that be the reason Huo-seng had left us? Had he been forced to as retaliation by the union? We would never know, but the idea struck us as plausible.

The status of Ding-chung was in no way diminished, Ralph discovered. If anything, he seemed more popular, more of a leader. He continued to play the clown, the stupid-canny person-to-make-people-laugh in the school entertainments, and always drew the applause.

In his spare moments, at sunset, he would play his flute. I would hear the five-scale minor notes drifting up from the garden, to wrap me round with a silver

Chinese gift atmosphere that seemed most appealing and appropriate.

In the coming months, Ding-chung, without his knowing it, was to help us in another way.

Ding-chung, caught in a trouble, without intending to, helped us see into the problems many of the students were facing.

At the end of the school year, Ralph asked him if he would return to us in the fall. He gladly promised to do so, and when fall came we welcomed him back. Almost at once we noticed a change. He was helpful as always, but less gay, definitely moody—so moody we felt concerned. In mid-fall, without explanation, he told us he was going home and took off for a week. We were puzzled.

When he came back, he was really in the doldrums. He was morose. The garden was neglected—weeds grew and the long row of potted yellow and bronze chrysanthemums dried from lack of daily watering. Ralph spoke to Robert Chen. The dean had mentioned his lower grades, wondering about the scholarship. I missed his flute, or if occasionally I heard it, the notes sounded melancholy. In spite of cautious probing, no one could find out the trouble. Robert said, "He is eating bitterness of some kind. It could be pressure put on him by some of the radical students who are still somewhat antiforeign. But I rather guess it is a home-side problem."

Ralph asked Ding-chung if he would prefer not to work for us, but he shook his head. That was not it then. We even wondered when he left to go home for the midterm Chinese New Year holiday if we would see him back. We worried and waited in suspense.

When one day near the close of vacation we saw him bounding down our steps into the garden, we breathed a joint sigh of relief. When we saw him actually smiling, we were overjoyed.

Ralph threw down his small hand trowel. "What has happened, Ding-chung? You look happy. Tell us, what has happened?"

"I found her a man." Ding-chung grinned broadly, slinging his bundle on the grass, his quick elfin face crinkling, eyes laughing. "I found her a man!"

"Good! Wonderful! Would you tell us who *her* is?"

So Ding-chung sat on a flat stone in the garden, and we sat on the stone bench while he told us the story that his pride had kept him from burdening us with while it was still unsolved.

When he was home the previous summer he told us his parents had broken the news to him that he was to be married soon. They reminded him he had been betrothed since childhood, in the usual manner, through a match-maker or "go-between" to a peasant girl of a neighboring clan, that she had grown up strong as an ox and would make him a good wife. The girl, because of her strength, was bringing a good price, and they needed her extra hands as his mother was in poor health due to worry caused by the bandits, who constantly moved back and forth in that area, and, from hunger, demanded food or they would burn the villages, or at least so they threatened.

He said to us, "*Ai-yah*, I told my parents, 'I will not marry ox. I am college man and have learned ideas more important.' I refused them, which meant they could disown me. That troubled me for I believe also in family respect. We have always been taught—family comes first."

His father, who had already sacrificed to send a son to school, finally told him he could return to college but the wedding would be held during the New Year vacation. Torn between his new ideas and his duties he decided to do a little reconnoitering. Maybe the girl wasn't so bad. Maybe…well, that week he had gone home, in the fall… he had gone to the girl's village, and with the help of a cousin of sorts, he had worked out a way to observe the girl, to look her over carefully as she worked in the field, without her knowledge.

He said, dropping his jaw and popping his eyes in mimicry, "A nong-giang she was. *Ai-yah*, a stupid! Imagine trying to talk with stupid like that about our country and our revolution! Imagine to look at her, rest of my life! I thought of pleasant-looking girls at our Wen Shan Girls' School with interesting minds and education like our college—and not bad to look at, also."

Ding-chung grinned with a hint of embarrassment as he continued, "I decided when I get married I choose my own wife. This is New Day, isn't it? This is part of revolution!"

Ralph said, "How did you work it, then? The betrothal had been made, and we've been told a betrothal is almost as binding in China as a marriage."

"Wait," said Ding-chung, putting all his dramatic skill into the act. "I tell you. But you could never believe how terribly I feel! Sick…sick in my stomach and mind. Well, I went secretly to see go-between. I tell him I will break the agreement. He is so angry for if I did this he will lose last part of payment from parents. I tell him my determination. Nothing could change my mind—even to be disowned. He begged and pleaded with me. Then I soften—oh, so little. I tell him there is one way—just one way. If he can produce a man to take my place, then I promise he will not to lose his fee. He agree, and before long he thinks of just the man—another cousin of sorts."

He continued, "This man is free—his parents have not the money, or will, to arrange marriage. He is man strong for pushing plow behind his ox, not man of ideas. A woman like this ox-girl can be real help to him. She is woman of the fields. Here is chance to get such strong woman with bride price, all paid for him. The go-between promise he will talk to this man and try to persuade him to the plan.

"I return to school here, hoping best but fearing worst. All I can dream is marriage to that girl if our plan does not work…or hurting my parents. You cannot guess what it is like to be 'outside family' in China. Like man lost on raft alone in rough sea."

Ralph said, "So that is why you were so upset those weeks. I don't blame you. How did you work it out?"

Ding-chung continued. "Those terrible midyear exams…I thought surely I will fail them. And then I thought, what matter…if I have to marry that girl life will be no use anyway. So I went home…New Year's…" He paused for the full effect, and we waited.

"Go-between tell me the man accepted! But now, hardest part, convince my parents! *Ai-yah*! To my joy they are most reasonable. So long as marriage will go through, they will not lose face. The girl will be coming to their house and will be help as it is cousin of mine she is marrying. I told them I will pay the final fee to marriage broker when marriage is complete. They are so happy to think they will not disown me, and they are proud to have scholar son. Everybody happy now!"

"What about the girl?" I asked, trying to grasp the intricacies of Chinese ways.

"Oh, no difference to her. And it is much more suitable match. Even go-between agree to that."

Ralph said, "I think you will go a long way, Ding-chung. I congratulate you on escaping marriage so successfully!"

They exchanged a sly wink, which I ignored.

"Just one more thing, if you won't think me rude for prying into your private affairs. How are you going to be able to pay this final fee? You are a magician, I know. Can you pull it out of that Chinese straw hat?"

Ding-chung airily tossed his farmer hat into the air and caught it in his old free manner. "That is all care for. I will save my four dollars month board money at the college dining room."

"But you have to eat."

"I cook my rice in your servants' kitchen. Never mind expensive trimmings. What do bite of pork and pickles matter when now I have my freedom?"

That evening we heard from the garden tunes as gay as could be played on a Chinese flute.

Part III

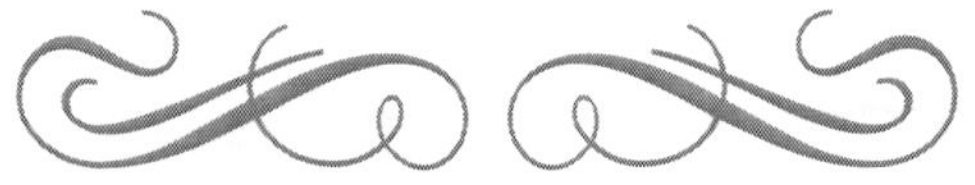

The Key

October 1928

Above the gate in the wall that separated our compound from the college I saw again the Chinese characters: "Foochow College: Scientific Institute for Learning." Today they both welcomed and frightened me. I was to teach my first class.

Turning the key in the wooden gate, hearing the ancient door creak open, I thought, at last…

My hand trembled as I slipped through and locked the door behind me. At last, after two impatient years, for an hour each day while the amah cared for my baby, I was a part of the college for which we had come to China.

Stone steps, uneven, treacherous, zigzagged down the hill—forty-six of them. I remembered counting them one day last year—that empty, deserted day in the silence of a closed school. Closed after a second fire had destroyed another building, and antiforeign demonstrations made school impossible. All the students had been sent away. How we despaired. How could we make friends with Chinese students in a revolution that left our dormitory and science hall blackened ruins, smelling of smoke and hatred?

But that was past—that was last year. Now in October of 1928 was a new beginning. The ivy-covered buildings on the hillside and circling a wide courtyard below reminded me that this school—the first for Western education in South China—had seen many kinds of battles since its founding seventy years before by intrepid missionaries. Now among the old buildings new ones faced the wide stone-flagged courtyard at the foot of the hill.

I could see the students coming out of its door as classes changed. How modern they looked in their starched blue cotton school uniforms with silver buttons, so different from their traditional Chinese long-coats they had worn until this year. Almost military—symbolic of the "New Day" they all talked about.

My heart pounded, and my throat was dry. Halfway down the hill in a battered building on my right was the room where I was to teach my first class in China—an incoming class in the senior middle school. This first class would involve more than the usual test of a first day of teaching. These boys, taller than me, were older than high school boys in America, and more politically conscious. I thought, *It will be a battleground. I'm a suspected foreigner—and only a woman!* Though the New Day preached equal rights for women, still the men secretly considered them of little importance except as they ruled in the home. My shortcomings overwhelmed me. Did I have anything to offer that they would consider important to their needs? How would they receive me? I was frightened. Feeling the key in my pocket, I longed to run back up the steps, but my feet carried me on.

I wouldn't expect the students to bow to me. They didn't bow to their teachers anymore, I had been told. For centuries pupils had always greeted their teachers with a waist-low bow. Now they bowed to Sun Yat-sen, the Father of the Revolution, they called him, whose picture hung on classroom walls. But to their teachers, if they so much as inclined their heads, it was all that could be expected.

There were other problems. How well Robert Chen had stated them in his report to the board of directors: "The buildings are in disrepair, the funds in arrears, faculty disrupted, the government suspicious, and the student's insubordinate."

It was only due to this man's determination, the loyalty of a few Chinese teachers, and Ralph's encouragement, that we were able to open at all.

Well, if we could build a school again out of the chaos of the past two years, I wanted to do my small part. It was the word "insubordinate" that worried me. However, if the students ran me out, I would have tried.

Entering the old building, I found my musty room with its marred desk, a painted wooden blackboard, and rows of benches with plain tables for desks. A blue and white picture of Sun Yat-sen, with his strong kindly face, stared down on the room from behind my desk.

Beneath the picture were two crossed red, blue, and white Nationalist flags.

On my desk I found a list of the pupils and a note: "Sorry, textbooks not arrived," signed by the dean.

I had a copy of the book we were to start with, a course in American literature especially prepared for use in China. I had planned that we would read aloud the well-written foreword. I thought, now what shall I do? The confusing Chinese names on the list blurred before my eyes, and the paper shook in my hands.

I sat, my mind blank, and waited. A bell rang. Boys entered and took their seats on the stiff benches… A dozen, fifteen, I counted. They did not rise to give me even a token bow or a look of recognition. I decided not to make an issue of it as some of the Chinese teachers had. After all, I was new to their ways. Their Asian faces looked alike to me. Their black hair, cut in the long style they favored, copied the modern haircuts of the radical students—the extremists, the trouble-makers. Were their narrow eyes hiding arrogance? I could not tell.

I stood before them—a reversal of custom—and spoke slowly, "I am going to call the roll. As you are hoping to learn English, so I wish to learn Chinese. If I make a mistake, will you correct me? And please stand so I can know more quickly who you are."

I stumbled through the list of Chinese names. The students did as I asked—they were polite but cold. I thought, as newcomers to the senior section of the school they were perhaps as uneasy as I. They were on their guard. Their defiant eyes said, "You are a foreigner. We don't trust you."

My knees were still shaking. There was only one thing to do—speak to them from my heart. I moved in front of the desk to be close to them.

"You have told me who you are. Now I will tell you why I am here. My husband and I have come to China to be your friends. You want your country to take its rightful place among the nations of the world. You will need to speak English. If we teach you English and other subjects, we want you to teach us about your people and your country. This is the modern way—we learn together."

They did not stir. I glanced at the picture behind me. "With you, we believe in the republic your leader, Dr. Sun, tried to found. But to build a democracy is difficult. It takes men of character and vision. You must be not only Chinese—you must become citizens of the world."

The faces before me were unresponsive, except for a flicker of agreement in the eyes of a sensitive looking boy in the front row. Had they understood? There was only one way to find out.

"Will you please stand, repeat your name, and tell me why you chose to come to Foochow College?"

One by one they rose and spoke haltingly. I was surprised to find their English was understandable.

"I come to this school to have modern education."

"I come to Foochow College because everyone know she is best school in Foochow. Government schools not so good."

"I come to learn the science—China must know the scientific method."

An agile boy jumped to his feet, pushed back a troublesome strand of hair, and spoke with feeling. "Ru-fu my name. I wish to help my country. China is swallowed up by Western powers. Western powers teach China one lesson—'might make right.' China must become strong nation. Must drive out Western powers."

A fireball, I thought.

Heads nodded. There was a murmur of approval. A round-faced boy, relaxed and easy-going, smiled as he rose. "Dai-hok my name. Chinese do not like Western powers but like American teachers to come and teach us the English."

Now they all smiled except one glum boy in front. He rose, staring at me rudely. "Gau-daik my name. I do not like Western school but must have Western education. Government schools not good enough. Imperialism is China's worst enemy. All China's troubles caused by West. Western schools must not be imperialist." I recognized the familiar line with his half truth. This boy was potential trouble.

The sensitive-looking student on the front row spoke. "My name Siu-ding. I think Foochow College is not imperialist. I come to this school to learn to be—what you say—citizen of world."

A tall boy with a scholarly face stood. "I am Ming-sing. Siu-ding is right. Old Chinese proverb says 'All under heaven one family.' Why must always be wars? Western nations should study Chinese teachings."

I glanced at Gau-daik. The haughty coldness of his face reminded me of the troublemakers who, we thought, had instigated the burning of our buildings.

At the close of class, I said, "For tomorrow write a paragraph explaining the term 'a citizen of the world.'" A risky assignment, I knew, in a land where Nationalism breathed hot and Communism smoldered under the surface.

The students left the room without as much as a glance in my direction. Had I been hoping for more? At least they hadn't walked out on me during the session. And they had talked about what was closest to their hearts.

As I turned the key in the wooden gate once more, I realized that for one hour I had completely forgotten my household problems, caught once more in the excitement of teaching. Could I lead them, I wondered, into thoughts deeper than the patriotic propaganda that was filling their need for a purpose in life? Could I help them find the key they needed for the China they would build?

The coming weeks and months proved to be a struggle parceled out in day-by-day challenges.

Soon the faces that had looked alike to me at first came into focus as distinct personalities.

Ru-fu, who sat in the center of the class, was plainly marked as a leader, for either good or ill. Wiry, emotional, and uninhibited, he would pour forth his thoughts in a fluent stream of mixed up English and Chinese. His father, I learned, was a member of the Nationalist Party. I could imagine Ru-fu on a street corner stirring up a mob.

His closest friends appeared to be Dai-hok and Ming-sing, for they came and went together. Ming-sing, tall, dignified, resembled a scholar of the old tradition. However his mind, I soon discovered, was not satisfied by rote learning in the ancient way. He liked to analyze every situation, both in politics and in the literature we were studying. He was a good balance to Ru-fu, I thought.

Dai-hok, round-faced, pleasant, was the class joker. When Gau-daik, scowling like a hot-tempered cook preparing a stew, stirred the simmering anti-Western feelings of the students, Dai-hok with a quick Chinese joke which I couldn't understand, always drew a laugh. I could understand the relaxing of the tension.

Siu-ding, younger than the others, was also the brightest. His papers needed few corrections. Fine looking, sensitive, I felt drawn to him, sensing that he wanted to be friendly but was afraid to show it because the times demanded certain hostility to anyone from the West.

Throughout the first term, the wall of suspicion, though it cracked apart now and then, remained a barrier between us. They did their assignments…except when they thought them too long or that I had been grading them too harshly.

Gau-daik and Ru-fu led the hostility movement. A daily test of my patience became their resisting eyes.

One day when I had returned some compositions, Gau-daik, leaving class, looked down on me with open arrogance. His paper had received a low mark.

"Someday we'll drive all the foreigners from China."

I couldn't see his eyes—they were closed…slits of anger. *Help me*, I prayed silently. *Help me to understand, to reach him. I am only one woman who has nothing to do with the arrogance of my countrymen who have caused so much suffering in China.*

I put out my hand and stopped Gau-daik. "Wait a minute. I want to talk with you."

He looked at my hand and then at me. His face was closed—withdrawn. "I will wait."

He stood there watching me sullenly as I put away my papers and the others left the room. He knew and I knew that my detaining him was a false bravado—yet I had to go on. I wished the bell would ring. When the others had gone, there was an echoing silence. I felt helpless. I looked up at his narrow eyes defying me.

"Why—why do you hate the foreigners so much?"

Gau-daik towered over me, smiling bitterly.

"For a hundred years the men from the West have had their gunboats in our rivers."

Not daring to face him, for I was afraid of his answer, I turned away and moved to the window from which I could see the city roofs beyond our compound. Slowly coming back, I said, "Is that why those soldiers out there are wearing bayonets? Are they for me? My husband? My countrymen?"

He responded, "You are the white man…"

The bell rang. He darted me a look and strode toward the door. There he turned and said, "White missionaries!" and left.

Trembling, I glanced down at my student record book on the desk. *I hate grades…how can we tell whether a human being is passing or failing?*

Scribbling my name savagely at the bottom of the page, I added a big round zero.

Despairing, I climbed the steps to our home, hating each crooked step. We must get to know them as human beings. But how…in a land so filled with propaganda… how? The answer was slow in coming.

Throughout the remainder of the day, as I fed my baby and put her down to nap, and sat at my crowded desk to grade papers, Gau-daik's angry eyes and tormenting words thrust at me. Was he being a spokesman for a majority of the boys? I felt he was. I longed for America—the pleasant home we had left, a student-campus ministry job Ralph might have had. And I saw again the hostile Chinese eyes of Gau-daik, Ru-fu, and a number of the others in my class. Hopeless to try to teach them, to befriend them in a revolution.

I couldn't wait to tell Ralph what had happened. When he came in late in the afternoon, I poured out my story. I, who almost never wept, felt my voice choke. "I hate it here. Let's go home."

Ralph looked at me, startled. "But we can't. We signed up for six years."

"Yes, we're missionaries. I hate the word as much as Gau-daik does. We're supposed to be good…but I'm not good. I'm afraid. And we're tools of imperialism, and they hate us. What earthly good can we be when they hate us?

Ralph started toward me, and I saw the distress in his eyes. But I pushed him away. His lips hardened, and I recognized his streak of stubbornness. Maybe it was his firmness—his strength. Now it seemed to me like stubbornness.

"They don't all hate us." His words were a plea.

I glanced toward the nursery. "Even if we all died—even our baby—you'd stay because you promised. *Missionary*!"

He winced and turned away. I had thrown at him all that Gau-daik had hurled at me. As he turned, I saw his eyes—how tired they were. Suddenly I realized he was suffering the same frustrations as I—his failures to reach some of the boys—and he had it all day, every day.

And now he had turned from me.

I couldn't stand separateness from him. Like a wind from some deep valley in my soul, a great shame started to fill me. But he had turned away. I heard his voice, cold.

"We'll go back to America—if that's what you want."

Disappointment—awful disappointment was in the drooping timber of his cold words.

I did not answer. Something was happening inside of me. I waited.

He spoke again. "Remember what we used to say. Missionary—it's only a word. It's what you put into it that matters."

I made one last appeal. "But I don't like the image—and I can't put a good content into it," I sobbed.

He turned, and pulling his clean handkerchief from his pocket, smiling he dabbed my eyes. “Partner, I didn’t marry Mrs. Matilda,” and he named a very upright English missionary we knew.

There was a twinkle in his eyes, we both grinned, and I felt his arm hold me close.

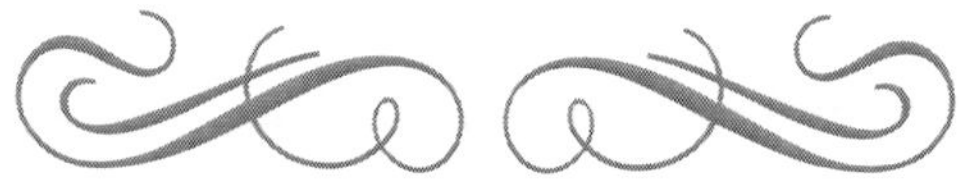

Canopy of Heaven

January 1929

On this day among the entire crowd, Ralph and I were, as far as we knew, the only foreigners. We had come to learn more about China—to feel a part of the people with whom we lived. Three of our college students were guiding us—like a bodyguard, I thought. What do they think of all this? Are they so westernized that their folk ways are as foreign to them as to us? It would be revealing to see it through their eyes.

Up the winding stone steps, above and below us, were coming all the people of Foochow, it seemed, to celebrate the Chinese New Year. Ahead of us rose Yu Hill—Canopy of Heaven—the roofs of its sprawling temples curved against the blue morning sky. Into our ears dinned a roar of excited voices mingled with the whining cries of beggars who squatted by the steps. Beyond the hill, I could see the gray stones of the massive city wall, protecting the city in its holiday mood.

I glanced at Ru-fu, Dai-hok and Ming-sing ahead of us—their foreign leather shoes, crisp blue school uniforms with silver buttons were sharp contrasts to the Chinese soft cloth shoes and long-coats of the city men. After three months of school, how little we knew what was in the minds of these boys with whom we worked every day. Communist ideas? Western teachings? The pull of their old family ways? All these at once caught in whirlwind changes? As they shielded us from the jostling crowds on the steps, their impassive faces told me nothing.

I glanced again at the beggars. Appalled by their numbers, I had been counting them. Fifty-six, Fifty-seven, Fifty-eight. Squatting close enough to touch us, whining their chants, they stuck out swollen legs so we could pity their red, open sores. They shook their gourd bowls, rattling coppers.

"Do good works. Teacher, Teacher's Wife, Students. Do good works. Heaven will reward."

Fifty-nine. Sixty. Ralph, following me, dropped copper coins in the bowls as I did from time to time, shuddering at the leprous hands and faces, the eyes that gazed at us without seeing.

The students shouted warnings to any beggar that threatened to grab my skirt or Ralph's trousers. "Get back. Let the foreign teachers pass."

I touched Ru-fu. "Don't do that. They won't hurt us."

The students were cold, I thought, hardened by long familiarity with sights of misery. In China begging was a profession allied with the Thieves Guild, and taken for granted. Could I ever become hardened to the blind, the maimed, to lepers by the hundred, in a land where no one seemed to care? I hoped I would not.

"Win merit—give a copper. Heaven will reward." The pleas pulled at my heart. Everyone knew that deeds of charity on the New Year brought luck for the entire year. Coppers clinked in the bowls.

At the top of the hill, the line of beggars ended, and we were caught in the jostling throng of holiday makers. What a clamor! At flimsy stalls hawkers called out their incense sticks, red candles, and gold idol-paper money for the gods. Men and women shrilled bargains. "Come buy, come buy." "How much?" "Ten coppers." "You rob us—and on New Year's Day. Here—give them to me."

Pushing through the crowd, the boys opened a way for us, not glancing at the booths. Foolishness, their manner said. I thought, *What does this mean to students of chemistry, physics, and philosophy?* I wished I could read their minds.

Ralph had discovered a few days ago that, due to bandit conditions on the Min River, some of the boys would be unable to return to their homes for the three-week holiday. He had suggested to them that we visit the temples together. They would become our teachers for the day, interpreting what we would see. They had accepted, and now they surrounded us protectively. But their manner was reserved, cautious, as it had been since the two college buildings had been burned the previous year. Were these boys antiforeign at heart? I could only guess.

Approaching a large Taoist temple with the crowd, through a side entrance, we were pushed along a narrow passage, almost crushed in the good-natured mob.

At last we burst out into the central hall of the temple. Acrid smelling, ear-splitting firecrackers banged on every side. Hundreds of people milled about before many idols, carrying out their acts of individual worship, assisted by shaven-headed monks in saffron robes. The hall was filled with a fog of eye-stinging smoke.

Gradually as my eyes, ears, and nose adjusted, I could see what was going on.

In the center of the high-pillared hall, a fire in a huge stone brazier was constantly fed by the worshipers. A man standing near me, holding a square of gilt idol-paper, lighted it from the flame, raised one foot in its black cloth shoe, twirled the burning paper three times under it, three times under the other foot, three times over his head, and dropped the burning paper into the brazier. Others were doing the same. The fire in the brazier leaped up, hot and crackling.

Women knelt on round, dirty mats before idol shrines. I watched a priest give a woman a bamboo holder containing inscribed bamboo sticks. She shook the holder gently, persistently, until at last a stick fell upon the stone floor. Her lips moved and I heard her plea, "Will I have a son, O God of Fortune? Will I have a son?" The priest picked up the stick and read the answer, without expression on his cold impersonal face. I saw the stricken look in the woman's eyes as she grabbed the container and started to shake the sticks again.

At another shrine a kneeling woman was throwing two oval wooden discs, which clattered on the stone floor. One side of each disk was round, one flat. Flat side and round side up—the answer is yes. Flat side and flat side up—the answer, no. Her eyes were pleading. "Tell me today—will I have a son?"

Across the hall, the large prayer wheel spun under the deft fingers of a monk, while an old man with waist-long whiskers stood by, his eyes hungrily waiting. The wheel slowed down, stopped, and the monk drew out the red card at the top, read the answer. The old man put coppers in the monk's hand, made three deep bows, while his granddaughter, in tight-fitting modern dress, nodded her head to the monk and pushed the old man gently on.

Moving along the hall, we passed an ancient stone turtle bearing on its back an inscription tablet. The turtle's head had fallen off and lay dejectedly near the shell. On a carved pillar hung an ugly Western clock, its brass pendulum swinging back and forth. But the clamor of the crowd drowned out its ticking.

It was a relief to leave the commotion of the temple and move out to quiet walks among smaller shrines. We were going to the far side of the hill where the great god Buddha still lived in his own peaceful courts.

Our students were talking in Chinese among themselves, and as I watched their clear young faces, I thought of their old religions—of Laotze, the founder of Taoism—the Road or the Way. I failed to see any connection between his profound mysticism and what we had just observed at the Taoist Temple. For the masses it had degenerated through the centuries to this—superstition and fortune telling rites. Could these students of modern learning believe in a religion of bamboo sticks, idol paper and prayer wheels? By the superior way in which they had looked upon it, it was obvious they did not.

Approaching the Buddhist temple, deserted on this day, we crossed a wide courtyard with a neglected goldfish pool. At the entrance we passed between high stalls from which four images, two on either side, leered down at us with grimacing faces. They made me shudder.

I turned to the boys loitering behind us. "Ming-sing, what is the name of the god with the sword and serpent?"

Ming-sing, scholarly and thoughtful, surely knew more about the temples than he admitted. He scrutinized the ugly images. "They have to do with the four winds of heaven, I think. Sorry, I cannot recall names."

I turned to Ru-fu, who glanced uneasily at the others, questioning them in Chinese. "We do not know...people think these idols guard temple."

I was disappointed. Were the boys hiding a kind of shame? I could not tell.

We moved to a large columned hall, its high beams carved in colors of gold and crimson, now blackened with smoke and grime. The students gazed up without expression at the large fat Laughing Buddha, his round stomach cracked, his paint peeling.

"What is his Foochow name?" I asked.

Ru-fu's face was cold. "Teacher's Wife, it is too long ago. We have not study these gods."

We reached the silent central court, where towering above the smaller *bodhisattvas*, followers of Buddha, sat the great Buddha, gazing vacantly out from his gilded lotus leaf. I looked at the boys. Their faces were as unrevealing as the god's. What of the Eight-Fold Path and the peace of Nirvana? Or the life of contemplation?

"What do you know about him?" I whispered.

"Only a little—a very little..."

"Do his teachings mean anything to the people?"

There was a long pause. Incense curled up from an urn in front of the god. A gong struck one bronze note and died into silence. From a distance came a murmur of monks chanting prayers.

Ru-fu said, "To the people—sometimes. To students—no."

Ming-sing added, "We know, but we have not words to tell. It is not important—for our world today it is not important."

With a cold indifference, they moved on.

Behind the great Buddha was the inmost shrine—to Chinese women, the holy of holies. In a high alcove, covered with traceries of lotus flowers and bamboo trees, stood a tall figure, the Goddess of Mercy—Kwanyin—friend of the suffering wife, the longing mother. Her garments flowed about her with delicate grace. Her face of compassion seemed to say, "I was once a woman. I understand..."

A woman was kneeling on a straw mat bowing at the foot of the idol. The white flower in her hair touched the stones each time she bowed. Every line of her thin body seemed to strain with her supplication, and as she lifted her eyes, I thought only great trouble could make them so hopeless, so pleading. What sorrow was she enduring? I wondered, knowing the many problems Chinese women had to bear.

She bowed a third time. Rising, she picked up a stick of incense from the floor and held it to a candle burning by the bronze urn on the altar. At last a tiny flame burst from it and settled into a steady glow, sending out a pungent fragrance. Sighing she planted the incense in the urn beside other sticks, now cold. The smoke drifted upward toward the face of the Goddess of Mercy.

Backing away reverently, the woman kowtowed once more, her face relaxed. She stood quietly at the back of the room contemplating her incense.

We moved closer to the shrine looking up at the goddess. Then I saw Ru-fu put his hand in his pocket. He pulled something out—could it be incense? A candle? And went to the altar. I held my breath as he leaned forward and remained motionless. Then I saw he had put a cigarette in his mouth and was waiting for it to light at the glowing incense the woman had placed there.

He straightened up, breathed out the smoke, looked contemptuously toward the woman, and moved back from the shrine. In his act he had knocked over the woman's stick of incense. The ashes in the urn immediately extinguished its glow.

My quick glance took in the students' arrogant faces and the narrowed line of my husband's mouth.

The woman stared at us with stricken eyes, and her voice choked, "Students! Foreigners!"

Ralph said gently, "Wait." Quickly he moved to the altar, relit the woman's incense at the candle flame, and set the stick firmly upright in the urn. He moved back, and we watched the incense burn again.

The woman glanced from the incense to Ralph, bewildered. She stared at him—at his face and clothes, and at the students standing there so still. Plainly she was puzzled. She gazed again at the burning incense. Slowly… slowly the anger faded from her face. It grew peaceful—as if she believed her prayer had been answered.

Putting her hands together, she raised her eyes to Ralph's and bowing from the waist repeated over and over again the Chinese words for thanks. Relief and gratitude filled her eyes.

Ralph said in Chinese, "Don't bow to me," and gestured to the altar.

She moved to the kneeling mat, dropped to her knees, and made three deep kowtows to the floor.

Ralph led the way from the room. His face was grim. The boys' leather heels clicked on the stone floor as they followed.

We left the temple in silence, walking down the wide stone steps to its outer court. To avoid the crowds and beggars our students led us around the far side of the barren hill by a path through boulders and yucca. On a knoll we discovered a small shrine sheltering a crumbling stone god. Before the shrine two seats invited travelers to rest and meditate. Here we stopped.

From our high point, we saw the thousand-year-old wall that surrounded the city. Its battlements were falling. Bushes grew from the cracks of its granite stones. On top of the wall, blue-clad workers scurried with wheelbarrows, or bent over, swinging heavy hammers. In time to their blows, they chanted a work song, and the *poon, poon, poon* of their hammers kept the rhythm.

Conscious of Ralph's silence, I said, "They are demolishing the city wall. Why are they doing that?"

Ru-fu, always the first to reply, said, "To modernize. They crush the rock to level wall into new road to go around city. The New Day!"

Ming-sing, whose long thin face and intelligent eyes gave the impression of a scholarly background, said, "The wall has to go. It belongs to the past. We students are doing the same thing—only we have rolled our past into a ball and kicked it into the sea."

Round-faced Dai-hok turned to Ralph with a grin and twinkle of mischief. "It's you foreigners have taught us to kick the ball."

I said, "Are all the old things so bad? What will happen without the wall when our war-lord, Lu Ting-bang, comes down the river with his bandits to capture the city again?"

Dai-hok grinned. "City will get big guns, I hope."

The boys laughed. Ralph, usually ready to laugh with them, did not smile. His eyes lifted from the city wall to the bandit country—distant Min River, a silver ribbon losing itself on the far side of the wide valley.

"You destroy the wall—so now in its place you get big guns!" Suddenly he turned to the boys. "Do you know the meaning of the word 'vacuum'?"

Puzzled they answered, "Empty…nothing…vacant."

Ralph said, "When you throw things away too quickly—when people throw away their past—it leaves a vacuum in their lives which will be filled—with something. What's going to take the place of your old ways—your old gods?"

"Science! Science!" The boys' eyes sparkled. "With science we can build modern China…industries…gun boats…modern weapons. We can defend against Japan and Western powers…"

Ming-sing added, "With science we build dams, control floods…no more starvation."

Ralph said, "So you make science your god. Science can also destroy the world."

"Not if you use science for good."

"If you make science your *highest* god, how will you guide men in using this power wisely?"

The students fell silent. Gazing from our hilltop, we heard again the poon of the hammers building the new road. The boys spoke together in low tones.

Finally Ming-sing said, "Choi Sinang, we are puzzled. You are Christian—you don't believe in idols. Why did you light the woman's incense for her in the temple?"

Ralph answered quickly, "You had frightened her. You had taken away her god. I simply tried to give it back to her."

Ru-fu's eyes narrowed angrily. "You succeeded. She went right back and kowtowed to her idol."

"But didn't you notice a change in her?"

Ming-sing said, "She smiled. Yes, she was grateful."

Ru-fu turned on him. "But she was bowing to Kwan-yin. That is superstition. The masses must be enlightened." His voice was full of scorn.

I saw the muscles tightening around Ralph's eyes and knew he was wincing at the arrogance. He had schooled himself—*don't preach at them…don't be imperialistic.*

"She's not a student like you. She's not ready to kick her past into the sea—not till you offer her something better. She belongs to her past. Yes, she returned to her worship—her security."

Ming-sing said, "When she went back to the altar she had a light in her eyes."

"You saw it. Her fear was gone—she found hope."

Ru-fu said, "Choi Sinang, how can China have hope without power? The Western powers have taught us 'Might makes Right.'"

There was a pause as Ralph looked at the boys, and I knew everything in him was crying out, *How can I speak to them*?

He turned aside and traced with his forefinger on the stone seat beside him the two Chinese characters for God, the Supreme Being.

At last he said, "Is that *all* they teach? What if four hundred million Chinese learn to hate—and to make modern weapons at the same time?"

I could see the idea growing in the boys' eyes.

Ralph continued, "Perhaps love, call it willed good, is the most important kind of power—of 'enlightenment'—there is. Without bandits would you need the wall—or the guns?"

We sat watching the figures on the wall…listening…hearing the pounding of the hammers. Behind us the bronze gong of the Buddhist temple boomed a call to worship, and from the distance drifted the faint clamor from the Taoist temple.

I looked at the temple roofs against the blue sky. Yu Hill—Canopy of Heaven—I thought—battleground of the gods…

Or was it instead, just possibly, a little mound of the Eternal? I glanced at the thoughtful faces of the boys and felt a surge of hope—even in Ru-fu's arrogance!

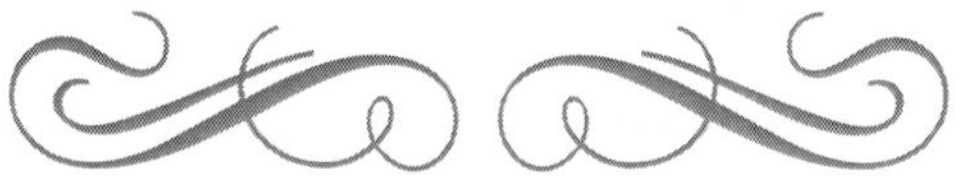

Bandits

February 1929

The conditions around us made their mark on our students.

When classes started after the New Year vacation, I missed Cho-sen, a short roguish boy, from his place in the back row of my class. When I inquired about him, the students shrugged.

"He did not return to school... We don't know... We told him not to go upriver—the bandits are too bad."

The dean said Cho-sen had not been heard from. "We warned the boys who have to travel in the country not to go."

A week later, I saw Cho-sen enter the room and rose to welcome him. He was emaciated, but his eyes snapped with excitement. He handed me a paper.

"My too-late composition," he said, grinning. "I am sorry to return to school too late."

This is the story he had written of his adventures:

> "I left Foochow on January 18. We rode in the armored launch up Min River that night, and

next morning we arrived at Ming Chang where two merchants and I got out and went ashore in the small boat. When we reached the village, it looked deserted. At once twenty-five bandits rushed out of the stores and captured the merchants, the boat people and me… After two or three hours walking (they took our watches so I don't know how long it was), we came to a village where we were to spend the night. Here I saw the first torturing of my fellow captives.

"I escaped the beating and other torture (too bad to describe) because I was a student, and because they thought of a better way to get the money from me. They made me address a letter to my father who is in the South Seas, and they wrote telling him they held me captive and that he was to send three thousand dollars ransom money…in mid-February most of the bandits left the village in order to get other captives. While they were away another group of bandits attacked us. When the attackers began to shoot, we captives lay down by the path. Our guards tried to make us get up but we refused, so they ran away leaving us exposed to the gunfire of the second bandits. We crawled into the mountain grass and hid there till night came. Then in night we traveled until we reached the home of one of the merchants who lived

> about fifteen miles away. I stayed at his home a day and then went across country and took a riverboat for Foochow."

In addition to the regular bandits there was much Communist activity about a hundred miles west of Foochow up the river. The landowners were robbed of their land, villages burned, and thousands of refugees streamed into the towns. One of my students wrote:

> "Some of our friends have sat in class during the last few days and wept because they fear their parents have been killed by the Communists. One boy knows his father has been killed."

There was trouble even on the outskirts of Foochow. The wife of a country pastor reported to the head of our mission:

> "One night last week after we had gone to bed, someone knocked at our door. We asked who it was and were told that a man had been severely burned. As my husband keeps a small stock of medical supplies on hand and tries to help the rural people when they are injured, they often come to him for help. We did not know these people, but they gave the names of friends of ours so my husband went with the strangers. I have not seen him since. They

> took him across the river and are holding him for ransom. Letters come telling me that he is being tortured and that he will be killed unless I send him the money. I have four little children and cannot raise the money."

Fear was the dark thread woven into the daily lives of our boys. Sometimes I wondered how they could study at all. Was it this fear, and the feeling that things did not have to be this way, that nurtured their compulsive desire to "save our country?"

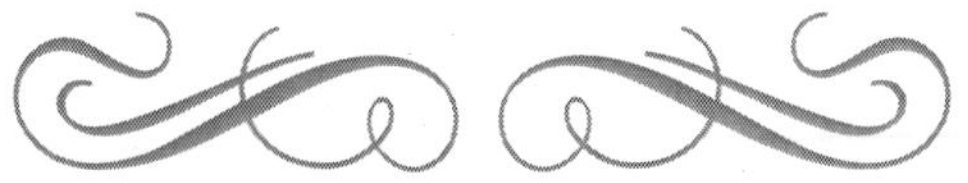

Students

Spring 1929

"Save your country from what?" we asked the students. From the bandits. From hunger. From corruption. From the West—its exploitation and China's humiliation. But how? By the new sciences?

There was an excitement in teaching Chinese students—in having a small part in the struggle of ideas that would affect the future of the world. Here, in the midst of student strikes, antiforeign demonstrations, Nationalism and underground Communism, we hoped to share some of the better aspects of the West.

We understood the vacuum left by the rooting out of their old religions and customs, and the explosive energy of the contending ideas rushing in to fill the vacuum. These boys were the spokesmen for the ninety percent illiterate of the land. They realized their power.

Daily we felt the tightening web of revolution. Could we do anything to justify our being here? We worked hard, but we didn't accomplish much. Nights when Ralph came home, I would see how weary he was and would think, we are only two people. Who do we think we are to make a difference? But his buoyancy always returned, and we would live another day of suspense.

Fourteen times that term the schedule was interrupted by demands for holidays so the students could demonstrate against the West, against Japan, against the government, or the school authorities. Government schools led the protests and pressured the Christian schools into compliance. If we did not comply, our students went on strikes.

One weekend our boys were allowed to visit the famous Kushan Monastery on a mountain fifteen miles from the city. On Monday they had not returned. When they came in twenty hours late, they said to the irate Chinese principal: "Yesterday it was raining. We couldn't see the scenery. It was necessary to stay over an extra day."

The faculty (all Chinese except ourselves and one other American) cut the deportment of every student one point and that of the leaders two points.

That evening there was a banging on our front door. A delegation headed by Gau-daik and Ru-fu confronted Ralph, their eyes angry.

Gau-daik said, "Choi Sinang, this is not right. We have student government. You helped us get it. Student government must decide punishment. We ask you now, go to faculty and tell them."

"Tell them what?"

"Tell them students must have right to decide. Or what good is student government?"

It was true that Ralph and our Chinese principal had set up a student council—something new in China. The dean, an old-school Chinese, had opposed it. "The students are putting themselves too high." But the principal and Ralph won.

So here was Ralph in a new role—middleman.

"You took advantage of your privilege. I'll speak to the faculty, but I can't promise anything."

Next morning at faculty meeting, Ralph, feeling it important to develop responsibility, urged that the problem be turned over to the students.

"There isn't enough leadership," the dean insisted.

"How else can we develop leadership if we don't let them use their tools?"

Ralph lost his case.

Three days later the whole student body met in the gymnasium. With shouts and jeers they voted to disband the student council. With set faces, the officers carried out their school constitution and all records and burned them. They watched the quick flames, the precious papers falling to ashes, and shouted till they were hoarse. Then they planned a non-cooperation movement. They brought pressure on the officers of the student council who resigned except for Ru-fu,the president.

The trouble spread to the dining room. Long dissatisfied with their cook, who, they said, was making too much "squeeze" by skimping on the bite-sized portions of meat, and substituting fish almost daily, the boys rapped on their bowls with chopsticks, shouting, "Down with the cook. *Dah-doh* the cook!" Stamping in rhythm, they chanted in mounting anger. Picking up a small plate of tiny fish portions from each table, they formed a line to the kitchen where they dumped the offending fish back into the cook's black kettle.

The Chinese faculty members tried to stop them, but the students brushed them aside. The boys shook their fists at the ashen faced cook, who grabbed his extra apron and ran out the back door. They demanded his resignation.

The whole school was tense, and for a few days, until another cook was found, it looked as if we would have to close the senior middle school again. The faculty took up the duties of the student organization and tried to ignore the noncooperation movement.

The Foochow City Commissioners, troubled by the growing power of students in all the schools, and wishing them to take their studies seriously, issued edicts prohibiting their demonstrations, which angered the students further. The Commissioner of Education announced that all seniors would have to pass a government examination to be given in all schools in the province. Immediately the government school students formed a union to protest. This spread rapidly. The union threatened all schools that did not join, saying that non-cooperating students would be stoned and beaten.

The union further declared measures would be taken against the commissioner himself if he did not change his policy, and that any principal who made his students take the proposed examination would be punished. In a neighboring city students took the Chinese principal, stoned him, and left him for dead.

The students in each school organized a vigilance committee to enforce the movement. They telegraphed other educational centers in the province, entertained newspaper editors, and placarded the streets to win the support of the people. Our own principal hired a bodyguard.

Finally a face-saving compromise was found—the commissioner promised that the government examination would cover only the last semester of work instead of the entire year. The students relaxed—and that problem was settled. But how long could schools stay open in such conditions?

Ralph and I knew that if we were to have any influence on the students we must try to see matters through their eyes. We continued to invite them to our home. They came evenings, two or three at a time, to talk to Ralph in his study. On weekends larger groups came to listen to our radio, play our record player, sometimes to play games, but mostly to talk. When I brought in tea and cakes, they settled on the floor around the fireplace. Gradually they began to speak what was on their minds.

"Choi Sinang, how can you call America a Christian country when they segregate people of color and sometimes lynch Negroes? Our papers tell us this."

Or "Western nations talk about wanting peace now. But they control the resources of the earth. I believe if they were in China's place, or India's, they would fight for their rights."

Sometimes the questions were about marriage:

"Which is worse—old style Chinese marriages arranged by parents, or Western style marriage with so much divorce?"

"Is marriage necessary at all? Why not free love?"

One boy said, "All the students talk about is, 'Eat, drink and marry, for tomorrow we die.'"

Another, "I don't know which is worse—old China or modern America."

The most popular subject was the political situation.

One evening six boys came, their hands full of leaflets. Dai-hok chuckled, "Look. Last night the Communists threw these into our school grounds. We got some before the faculty picked them up."

Ru-fu, his eyes troubled, said, "By night it's Communism. By day, Nationalism. Our old people tell us to respect the old ways. In the Christian schools, we hear about Christianity. How do we know what to believe? Here, read this."

He handed us each a leaflet. I read, "Students of the Christian Schools, you have been denationalized. If you do not wake up you cannot be counted as citizens. Wake up! Wake up quickly! Turn back to your country!"

Ru-fu asked, "Are we being denationalized?"

"You say you want to live in a modern world. Do you want modern agriculture? Modern science? Modern medicine? Is that being denationalized?"

Ru-fu took back the yellow sheet. "Sometimes I think Communists right. They not only talk—they act!"

There was silence. The boys stared at him. Communism was a dangerous subject. Since Chiang Kai-shek's split with the Communist party, anyone suspected of party connections could disappear in the night. It had happened to a few university students.

None of our boys were Communists to our knowledge, though some might belong to the secret cells everyone knew to exist. The danger was not imaginary. Chiang Kai-shek was sending armies to liquidate the roving guerrilla bands in the hills west of Foochow and the adjoining provinces. Cities only a hundred miles from us had been taken and retaken, leaving burned villages, ruined land owners, the homeless and dead. It was all coming very close.

Ralph was always asking, "Why?" He said, "I am an outsider. I came here hoping to understand China. Why do *you* think the Chinese for a century have hated the Western nations?"

At a gesture from Ralph, the boys sat down, but they did not relax. Their sharp voices cut the air of our peaceful living room interrupting each other with the old, but legitimate, grievances:

"The white men were barbarians. They forced their way into our country with their gun boats."

"We didn't have big boats or guns."

"Our emperor asked them to leave, but they refused."

"They forced unequal treaties on us—made us pay large indemnities."

"They took best parts of our cities for their own use."

"They forced us to trade with them and controlled our tariffs. We had no protection against their industries. They got rich using our cheap labor."

"They build parks and put of signs saying, 'No Chinese allowed.'"

"They set up their own law courts."

Ming-sing said, "But most of all it was the look in their eyes."

"Some white men," Dai-hok corrected. "Only *some*." He jumped up grinning. Then he strutted across the room, swinging an invisible cane, looking down his nose and switching imaginary Chinese out of the way. The boys laughed and clapped at his mimicry. But I saw Ralph's grimace and knew he was thinking of the walking sticks we carried in the villages sometimes because of the mangy dogs.

As others see us, I thought again. But now, at least, they were letting us laugh with them.

Ralph picked up one of the propaganda sheets. "All right. Go on. What's the appeal of Communism to the peasants?"

"Promises!" the boys chorused. "And after the promises, they divide up the land for the poor."

"Why does it appeal to the intellectuals?"

Dai-hok grinned at Ralph. "The Communists promise to drive out the Western powers. And build a strong China."

"The intellectuals have to lead the peasants." Gau-daik waved another rice-paper sheet. "Listen to this. 'In a very short time...several million peasants will arise like a tornado...a force so swift and violent that no power will be able to suppress it.'" Gau-daik's voice was loud. "'They will break all trammels that now bind them and push forward along the road of liberation. They will send all imperialists, warlords, corrupt officials, local bullies and bad gentry to their graves.'"

Gau-daik glared at the others as he sat down.

We examined the sheet. It was signed "From the report of Mao Tse-tung, 1927."

Ralph said, "Do you think this will happen?"

Ming-sing frowned. "Communism is an idea. You can't kill an idea with guns."

Ru-fu pointed at the rice paper sheets on the floor. "It's more than an idea. It's an organization with a plan of action and targets—the landlords and the Western nations."

Gau-daik jumped to his feet. "I come from up-country. The people have been so hungry they say, 'Nothing can be worse—we'll try anything,' and they grab the land the Communists give them. That's what they want—land!"

"They don't know they'll lose their freedom," said Ming-sing. "They've never asked, 'What is freedom?'"

"Have you?" asked Ralph.

They were thoughtful. At last Ru-fu spoke. "We have. We've studied the Republic Sun Yat-sen was going to build. But now neither Chiang Kai-shek nor the Communists give freedom."

"What is freedom? And how do you get it?" Ralph persisted.

The concentrated faces around us were shadowed by more than the light from the fire.

"Always push back." Ralph was relentless. "How did the concept of freedom within government develop?... How did the Communists in China start?...What is their objective?...Is that your objective?...If not, what is?...Will hate and bloodshed accomplish your ends?... Some of you have said that hate creates more hate. Will that bring freedom?...China is changing. How will you shape it?"

Ralph continued, "You have suffered. You are now in the heat of your Nationalism. Can you use it constructively?"

Ming-sing replied, "You tell us it must be stepping stone to Internationalism. Modern China must learn to live with world—or we'll all be destroyed."

The boys, except Gau-daik, nodded.

When they were leaving, Dai-hok gathered the rice-paper sheets and handed them to me. "You'd better burn these. If they found them in our rooms..." Drawing his hand across his throat, he grinned. I shuddered. Sometimes at night we had heard the sound of rifles firing on the Parade Grounds beyond the White Pagoda. By night it became the Execution Ground. I burned the rice-paper sheets.

Out of this session there developed a happening we never would have believed possible. Because of the deepening interest the boys expressed in serious matters, Ralph decided to expose them to the problems of simply staying alive as experienced by some groups in Foochow.

He had a class called social ethics—a substitution for the former courses in religion which had been banned by the provincial government. In the spring term he assigned each student a paper on what he would do if he were the commissioner of the City in Charge of People's Livelihood. Then each week during the spring semester, with permission from the authorities, they went on a field trip.

They visited the sampan workers, living in the small boats bumping sides on the Min River headquartered near the Bridge of Ten Thousand Ages. They went to the rickshaw pullers' headquarters where the pullers, many of them racked with TB and weakened by opium, came to pay their day's fee for the day's hire of a "man-pull-chair." Often the fares collected were not enough to pay the fee. Then to a soap factory and to a hosiery factory where listless children bent over their work in the whir of unguarded machines, and where working hours extended from before dawn to after dark. Girl children were cheap and expendable. The stench of the dormitories and the pallor of the children's faces made the students sick.

"Let's get out of here," one said. On the way home, they were silent until they reached the quiet lane approaching our compound.

Sui-ding said, "It's slavery."

"No," said a boy from a well-to-do family. "It's economic necessity."

Ming-sing said, "Choi Sinang, you have talked to us about worth of individual man, and human rights. How can you believe in a just God?"

Ru-fu looked at Ralph defiantly. "How can you believe in God at all?"

Ralph said, "Ask yourself, 'What is your concept of God? Does it need to grow?'"

Out of these experiences, discussions on religion grew spontaneously. Frequently our living room was the scene of heated debate—what a confusing tangle of ideas from the divergent backgrounds, none of which the boys understood.

Questions like: "Is religion really necessary? Russia says it is the 'opiate of the people.'"

"'Down with Confucius' is what the intellectuals say today. Confucius has kept China's eyes on the past—it has held us back."

"Buddhism is for the monks in the monasteries. It is religion of escape. No meaning in scientific day."

"Taoism? Look how they throw the fortune sticks in the temple and spin the prayer wheels. Superstitious practices. It is for the masses."

I recalled what we had seen when the students took us to visit the temples on Yu Hill, and how they admitted they did not know much about the religious backgrounds of their land.

I asked, "Have you studied about Buddhism and Confucius and Lao-tzu?"

They shrugged. "Today it is not important."

Ralph said, "You've heard the popular injunction, 'Study all things. Hold fast to that which is good.' Doesn't that apply to your own past as well as to what we call Christianity? Are you sure the Confucian code should be entirely scrapped? Or that all religion is outmoded?"

"It isn't practical today," Gau-daik shouted. "Christianity hasn't succeeded either."

Ralph gestured toward the city. "You mean it hasn't been practiced. Let's distinguish between the word 'Christianity' and the actual teachings of the Old Testament prophets and Jesus. What did the prophets say about justice and righteousness? What did Jesus teach about God and man? Look. You are writing a paper about conditions in Foochow. If you took the teachings of Jesus seriously what would you attempt to do?"

The boys challenged him. "We don't know anyone like that. Show us someone—someone today—a Chinese."

Ralph pulled his small date book from his pocket and thumbed the pages. "I know someone—I think we could get him—from North China. How would you like to have a conference next fall and invite the students from Wen Shan? We could begin to plan now."

Ru-fu said, "You mean a conference with girls coming? Girls aren't interested in these matters."

"How do you know they aren't? Have you talked with them?"

The boys looked at each other. Co-education was unknown. Since 1911 girls had taken part in demonstrations but never had students in Foochow held a joint conference or worked together.

Dai-hok's round face broke into a smile. "If girls come to talk with boys, I think ancestors will be unhappy."

"Not only ancestors. If my parents hear of this, they take me from school."

Siu-ding's sensitive face lighted. "But it is New Day. I think we do it." The others listened to him.

Ming-sing who saw around every situation said, "Radical students from government schools could take over and shout their antiforeign propaganda."

Ru-fu pushed back his long hair. "No, we will keep it small—just our school and Wen Shan. This is Foochow College first conference. We must make it success."

The hot-headed Ru-fu! Ralph smiled. You never knew which side Ru-fu would take—but if he favored a thing it was as good as done.

I watched Gau-daik's glum face. The number one troublemaker—would he be with us or against us?

"You've started something." Ralph was pleased. "Let's get on with it."

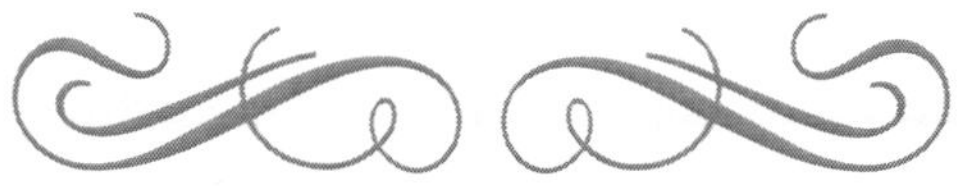

The Conferences

Fall 1929

The First Conference

There was no time to lose as school would be closing for the summer vacation. The next week twelve boys and girls from Foochow College and Wen Shan High School met in our living room. Ralph told them that the students were to run this conference. They were to choose the questions they wished to discuss, the leaders they wished to invite, and the procedures.

The girls, embarrassed in the presence of boys, put their hands to their mouths, giggled, and whispered their suggestions to their teachers. But soon they forgot the old taboo, and their cheeks flushed, their eyes shone. They argued as freely as American young people.

They decided to invite the speaker from the North, a prominent Christian leader. And Foochow's new Commissioner of Education, a Chinese educated in America. They did not want long speeches. They wanted time to discuss their problems with these leaders, and to exchange ideas with other students. The problem was to prevent trouble from anti-Western propagandists.

"We'll take care of that—we'll run out anyone who talks against our schools," they said.

"We'll have police at the gates," Ru-fu promised.

The conference was scheduled for November 1929. As rumors spread that it was to be co-educational, some of the older Chinese were distressed, and some of the Americans shook their heads.

"The boys and girls of China aren't ready for this. Not yet. They'll fall in love and all sorts of things happen."

Ralph smiled and stood his ground. "They have to learn to live in a modern world. The New Day is here."

He knew the risk. However, the values could be great—the conference could provide a constructive outlet for the energy and fervid patriotism of the students, and be in line with Western and Christian education.

Ralph's dream came true. This conference turned out to be a complete success. There was no trouble. Gau-daik and his friends remained silent—at least for the moment.

Even the older missionaries and Chinese breathed with relief and admitted it had done no harm.

The Big Conference

Now, buoyant with success, the students plunged into plans for a second—a bigger and better—conference for all the Christian schools in the Foochow area. With a year to plan, they would do something that would make its impact on the whole city. They would invite the six city commissioners and perhaps encourage them to try to correct some of the evils of the city. The Commissioner of Education backed them, saying he hoped their conference would set a pattern for the government schools.

During the spring and fall of 1930, with the energy of the students channeled, we could see the insubordination lessen and school spirit blossom.

In our home the committees' planning sessions turned into hot forums, debating which leaders to invite, which subjects to deal with. The words "military power" played through their talk like blades of steel, and the theme of democracy lighted their eyes. Religious questions rated second. Excitement mounted.

The brilliant October sun illuminated the eager faces of the students hurrying up and down the steps in their final preparations for the weekend of the twentieth. Carefully chosen committees wrote publicity for the local paper, made placards for the streets, and signs for the grounds and rooms. They planned each detail of the large assemblies for the addresses by the Commissioner of Education and the speaker from the North, and they selected the meeting places for the discussion groups. They printed a program. All the Christian middle schools in and around Foochow were to take part. A few representatives from the large government schools were invited.

The publicity stirred up the government school students who distributed leaflets and put up placards in the streets attacking the Christian schools. The eyes of the educational world and the local government were focused on the conference.

As if this were not enough, I had my own personal excitement. At the small mission hospital adjoining our compound our son, Whitney, was born on October 17, in the care of Dr. Lau, a Chinese woman trained in Western medicine. I had only a bedside seat to the events that were to follow. I pieced together what Ralph told me.

He ran in to see me Friday afternoon as the college compound was filling with boys and girls arriving by foot and by rickshaw from across the city. Police were at the gates to avert troublemakers.

Ralph, smiling down on his new son, said, "Keep all your fingers and toes crossed," and hurried away.

It was the extremists within our school he feared the most—the small group headed by a senior, Lo-chen, aided by Gau-daik. Ru-fu? We could not be sure. Though chairman of the conference, he had quarreled with the dean who had curtailed his power as president of the student council. This was a perfect opportunity for the radicals to unleash their propaganda and bring the conference down in ruins, throwing a shadow over all our schools.

It was late Friday night when Ralph tiptoed down the darkened corridor to report, "It's going great guns—you'd think they'd had conferences since the Boxer Rebellion."

"In a way they have. What about Lo-chen and Gau-daik?"

"They came. They sat on the front rows with their friends. They were very quiet—I don't know what's brewing. Keep your fingers crossed some more."

All day Saturday I waited, admiring my healthy boy and wondering what was happening. The day was long. I thought about my son—and those students out there—what kind of a world would they make of it? How might it affect his life?

It was late evening when a messenger delivered a scribbled note from Ralph: "Sorry, can't come. I am sitting on lid!"

So there was trouble. The night seemed endless.

Sunday passed slowly, and my bones ached with waiting...Ralph came late that night to tell me.

Saturday morning the conference had moved along as planned. The faculty members were impressed by the eagerness of the student's participation, the enthusiastic ovation they had given the commissioner after his address, and their heated but controlled discussions in the small groups.

A stand-up luncheon of rice and vegetables was served in the college courtyard. As Ralph was finishing his belated bowl of rice with chopsticks, some boys led by Siu-ding came running to him.

"Choi Sinang, come to the dormitory quickly!"

"Why?"

"Trouble. They're planning to break up the afternoon groups. Hurry." "Is Ru-fu there?"

"Yes—but hurry."

Ralph had always encouraged the student council to settle their problems. But now he ran across the courtyard and up the stairs.

In a dormitory room, he found a dozen students standing or sitting on beds. Ru-fu stood by the window, his face a mask. Lo-chen and Gau-daik, flushed, were talking in excited Chinese. When they saw Ralph they were silent…there was a hush. Gau-daik's whole demeanor changed. He dropped into a chair and wiped his face as if he were very tired.

He said sullenly, "I can't go to the meetings. I'm feeling sick."

Ralph faced him. "Is that the way you set an example for the others?"

The boys watched, their faces impassive.

Gau-daik wiped his forehead again with a limp hand. "I've made my sacrifice. I'm through with the conference."

Ralph looked at his watch. "It's almost time for the assembly to start. Do you think this is the right attitude to take?" He looked at Ru-fu. "You are presiding."

Ru-fu did not move.

Lo-chen said, "We got a holiday. That's all we wanted."

"So that's it—that's all you want—a holiday! How are you going to 'save your country' with holidays?" Ralph felt the blood rush to his head, choke his voice—Ralph who had disciplined himself so carefully never to be an "Imperialist." He was aware of the startled eyes upon him. He thought, *Whatever happens, this time I've got to tell them!*

Glancing around at the boys, some of whom he had come to know so well, he saw that now they appeared to be ready to follow their leaders, whatever destructive measures Lo-chen and Gau-daik chose.

Ralph said, "Is that your philosophy of life, 'holidays'? Please tell me why you are doing this?"

Gau-daik leaned back in his chair, Lo-chen watching him. "The conference isn't interesting. You told us it would be built around the Commissioner of Education. Now you have your Christian leader from the North give the afternoon address. You are trying to denationalize us—make us sympathetic to the West." He paused.

"Go on," said Ralph.

"All right, I will go on." Gau-daik jumped up. "I'm not interested in your god…your talk of willed good and peace! We need weapons—modern weapons—we should be fighting the West, and Japan, getting back what they've taken from us. I'm not interested in your conference." He glanced around the room, scowling. "Let the others go if they want. We want guns!"

Sui-ding, his face pale, confronted Gau-daik. "Tell him…tell him what you are planning to do. Tell him you are going into the discussion groups after the assembly and *dah-doh* (down with) the imperialists and the Christian schools, and break up the whole conference. That's what they're planning."

Lo-chen pushed Siu-ding aside. "He's right. We'll break up the conference, destroy the Christian schools, and drive out all the foreigners and their running dogs. Just give us time!"

Gau-daik said, "We'll start today."

The room swam before Ralph's eyes. He saw Ru-fu start to speak but silenced him.

"Listen to me. For more than two years, we've worked together. I've taken trips with you so that we might learn together. I've taken you to visit the factories, the rickshaw guilds, the sampan workers, to help you see your country—to get the social point of view to understand and help your country. I've given you books and spent many evenings discussing your problems. I've brought the best men to our school so you might hear them and know them. You told me yourself, Gau-daik, that the Chinese people would never learn to cooperate. And now *you* act this way."

Ralph paused. No one stirred. The boys' eyes were on him.

Thinking this is the end of everything we've tried to do, he continued, "A lot of us have worked from six in the morning till midnight to make this conference a success. Now you stand there and tell me you can't do anything unless it's interesting. Remember this: if you—we—built hate on hate, the world will destroy itself—including China. That would be interesting, perhaps. Where will China end if that's what her leaders do? What kind of a leader are you going to be? Another warlord?"

In the silence that followed no one moved. Ralph thought, "I'm being an Imperialist." He stood waiting—waiting for them to shout, to strike, to push him out, to cry "*dah-doh* the foreigners!" He was ready for anything—anything except what happened.

Ru-fu faced Gau-daik, his hands clenched. "Get out. Get clear out. We are students, not soldiers. Let them use the guns. We have to use our heads."

Gau-daik gazed around the room, at one and then another of the boys, as if waiting for a sign. There was none. His haughty manner dropped away. He shrugged then spoke. "Well, you heard. All right for now. What are we waiting for? It's late. Let's go to the conference." Gau-daik motioned to the door and led the way. The others followed. Ralph walked behind, scarcely believing as the whole group hurried across the stone courtyard to the assembly hall.

Ru-fu, presiding at the assembly, told the students that the eyes of all Fukien, even of Nanking, were upon their conference, this new experiment in the Student Movement. Its success or failure would prove the success or failure of students as leaders of their country—that China had it in its power, someday, to destroy the world, or to build a better world. The students applauded long and heartily. The commissioner nodded his approval. Ralph sighed and wiped his forehead.

That evening, however, he remained at the college till he was sure that the insurrection was over.

Following the conference, the newspaper publicity was favorable. The Commissioner of Education wrote a letter to the paper publicly commending the students. He wrote Ralph that he hoped to set up a similar conference for the government schools, though he feared the extremists would take over and run the show.

Ralph considered the conference a turning point in his relations with most of the students. Gau-daik and Lo-chen had lost their hold on the majority.

❋ ❋ ❋

Later that winter of 1931, the six city commissioners were kidnapped by a power-seeking faction, taken into hiding somewhere out of the city, and hid for weeks. We did not know whether they were alive or dead. Eventually five of the six were returned to their jobs.

In the spring, as our students were taking their exams, the warlord, Lu Ting-bang, tried to capture the city. He did not succeed as his guns were small, though several sections of flimsy wooden shops and homes went up in huge crackling fires. The ancient stone firewalls between sections prevented a complete conflagration. I watched the fires from our balustrade at the back of our house. Having been warned that we might have to run, I had two baskets packed for the babies.

The Japanese made further inroads in North China.

We read of terrible floods in the Yellow River Valley—of this we were to hear more later.

So we lived and worked in the midst of unease...and frequently I asked myself—why are we here?

But at the same time that I was feeling its sufferings, I was beginning to love China.

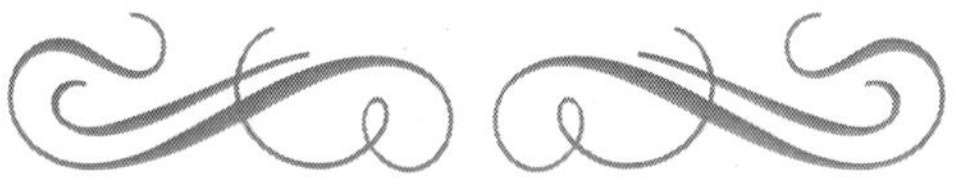

Su-sieng

February 1931

The worst things always happened when my husband was away—or so it seemed, the four years we had lived in China…like the typhoon that blew off part of our roof one summer and the day when I'd come down the mountain without him just before Ka-trine was born…

Now it was the Chinese New Year long holiday, and Ralph was away again—at a teachers' meeting. How I missed him.

Outside the walls of Foochow, bandits harassed the villages. Within the city, antiforeign agitators kept the people fomenting with propaganda. We never knew what slight incident would blow up a tornado of fury against the white residents—or frighten our most loyal servants from us—I slept on the edge of my bed.

And then one day Su-sieng came to live with us. It was against the rules—servants in American compounds could not bring their families, but Ai-nuk (Precious Jade), my child's amah, brought her child, Su-sieng, anyway.

It was the second day of the New Year. Chinese firecrackers were still popping outside our gate when Ai-nuk finally returned after several days off. I'd been watching all morning, thinking, she can't do this to me—she promised to come. The baby wash had piled up; we'd not had water in the supply jars for two days. Our regular cook and boy were away for three weeks to celebrate, so that morning the labor union had sent us a shifty-eyed substitute cook and his helper. But I needed Ai-nuk.

It was late afternoon. I'd almost given up when I saw her coming from the gatehouse carrying two round baskets. Then I noticed beside her a child in a bright flowered dress skipping up the hill swinging a small basket. *The amah bringing her child! But she can't do that!*

I saw the brightness in the girl's face and heard her laugh as she stopped to gaze at a mynah bird scolding from the banyan tree. As they neared the porch, Ai-nuk whispered, "Remember your manners." The child grew solemn.

To me the amah said, "This is Su-sieng. She's going to spend the rest of the holiday with me…here. We went to get her school books." Her eyes clearly defied me, as they had every day of the past months.

"But Ai-nuk…you know the rules…"

As I hesitated, Su-sieng put her hands together and bowed. "Peace-peace, Teacher's Wife, make the New Year." She looked at me, her large eyes pleading.

What a lovely child, I thought.

The amah took Su-sieng's hand and moved swiftly across the porch to my little girl tottering on her toes in a bamboo playpen. "Su-sieng, this is Ka-trine. Ka-trine, this is my girl. You'll be friends."

Su-sieng kicked off her shoes and climbed inside the pen, tossing Ka-trine a rag doll. They both laughed.

I thought, *Ka-trine will love this. Whatever can I do? Enforce the compound rules and increase Ai-nuk's hostility? Or forget the rules for three weeks and win Ai-nuk?* Somehow my child's amah, closest to me, had become a symbol of all China. I wanted desperately to be at home in this land to which we had chosen to come with the dream of making friends with the Chinese people. In many ways it had been a hostile land. Perhaps the child would be a bond between Ai-nuk and me...between China and me.

I had no one to consult. The three older men of our compound were away at the teachers' meeting with Ralph.

Reluctantly I said, "Come in, then."

Ai-nuk's face relaxed. Picking up her baskets, she carried them to the small room off the back verandah.

Su-sieng, Small Sprite, was well named. The following days she romped with Ka-trine up and down the hill, tossed her a bean bag, rolled her a hoop, and taught her to jabber Chinese words. After lunch, while Ka-trine napped, Su-sieng disappeared into our back garden with a book. During these days I saw a glow in Ai-nuk's eyes whenever they rested on her daughter.

There was one incident. Shiftless Ne-dee, our substitute cook's substitute helper, carrying water buckets up the hill from our well, stopped to gaze after Su-sieng. I heard Ai-nuk, from the pavilion, shout angry Chinese words at him. Ne-dee slowly turned and sullenly resumed his water-carrying. Ai-nuk was dividing her attention between my child and hers. Nevertheless I was glad I let her keep the child, and to my joy the amah's animosity to me lessened.

So two weeks passed.

Then, in the middle of a freezing cold night, my sleeping porch light flashed on, waking me. I thought fearfully, *What now*?

By my bed stood Ai-nuk. She was trembling. She whispered hoarsely, "Wake up, Sinaniong. Wake up, Teacher's Wife."

I sat up, shivering in the icy air. "What's wrong?" Instinctively I glanced out…no red glare in the sky—not another fire, or battle, or mob.

"My little girl…she's sick."

For an instant I felt relief—a sick child would get well. "What's the matter with her?"

"Trouble! Bad trouble!"

"What do you mean?"

"Come see for yourself…and in your house, too!"

Fumbling for my robe and slippers, I stumbled after her through the dark bathroom and out to the back verandah which led to her small room.

She pointed to the lower floor. "Be quiet. Don't wake the others." The cook's and boy's rooms below were completely dark.

In Ai-nuk's room a dim bulb burned. Her little girl lay huddled under the quilt on the amah's rattan bed, her face flushed, her black braids mussed. She was sobbing at intervals in a disturbed sleep. I felt her forehead…she was feverish. Pulling back the quilt, I saw that her knees were drawn up and her hand pressed low against her body. "It must be her stomach."

Swiftly snatching something from the table Ai-nuk glared at me. "Stomach…no! Not her stomach. She's been hurt…"

I recognized the Chinese phrase, "hurt to the death," as the amah flashed before me a pair of the child's blue cotton under-trousers matted with mucous and blood. I stared in disbelief. The implications crept gradually into my numb mind.

"But it couldn't be…she's only nine year's old."

"Yes, nine years old! It couldn't be…but it is!"

My knees gave and I sat on the edge of the bed. I felt a tremor of the child's body as she sobbed again. "Who did this?"

Ai-nuk glared at me. "Maybe you can find out. She won't tell me. Whoever did it said he would kill her if she told. I've known something was wrong for two days. Now she can't hide it any longer… It happened down there." She pointed to the servants' quarters below.

I was shaking in the awful cold. "Maybe she will tell me."

"Go ahead…ask her."

"Now?" I looked at the sleeping child, and at Ai-nuk, realizing for the first time that she was fully dressed. "What are you thinking of? We must get her to the hospital."

"Hospital! No! I'm going to get my relatives."

"Your relatives? Why?"

"My family—of course. But first I must be sure who did it."

That idiot boy! I shuddered.

The girl was stirring, and I talked to her gently. "Su-sieng, tell me. Who hurt you? Was it Ne-dee?" She clung to me. "Don't be afraid. I'll take care of you. Tell me, was it Ne-dee?"

She opened her eyes, glazed with fever, and then she wept. I stroked her head until she was quiet.

"Get me the sleeping pills and aspirin, Ai-nuk. And some water…"

When she returned, I raised Su-sieng's head but the amah pushed me aside. "I'll give it," she said, and I felt, as I had so often, her bitter resentment.

I had only one thought—to get Su-sieng to the hospital—but Ai-nuk said, "No. If we move her, Ne-dee and cook would wake up. If Ne-dee did it, he would suspect trouble and run away. But perhaps it wasn't Ne-dee." Her eyes, red from weeping, glared at me. "Perhaps it was a *Huang-giang* (a foreigner)."

Ai-nuk! You can't think that!" Her accusation horrified me. I thought of the four fine men who lived in our compound. "Anyway you know the Americans have all been away the past week."

As if she hadn't heard me, her voice choked. "The time will come when there won't be any foreigners in our land to hurt us. I'm going now."

I was frightened. "But why your relatives? Why don't we call the police? This must be handled through the law."

Her face was contorted with grief and anger. "No… you don't understand. We don't have *your* kind of law." I felt the sarcasm of her words. "We'll take care of this—the Chinese way. They'll find out who did it. You take care of her…and if anything more happens…"

"Ai-nuk, listen to me…" I started up, but she was gone.

Trembling in the cold, I leaned over to tuck the quilt closely about Su-sieng. Then I sat by her, and when she slept soundly, I crept back to my bed. Through the thin partition, I could hear her if she cried.

I tried to think, but everything was a jumble. I imagined the weeping amah jogging on her long rickshaw ride through dark Chinese streets to her village beyond the city walls. A three- or four-hour trip—she might have to walk the last freezing mile or two—blaming us, I knew, and planning her revenge each hard cold step of the way.

No sounds came from the room beyond mine—at least Su-sieng could sleep. The thought of this child being raped and infected revolted me. I trembled again and again in the cold sheets. What will happen? What can I do? Will the relatives kill the boy?

Vividly I imagined the murder of the boy in our house…

Then a new fear drove out the first—might not the relatives, blaming us Americans, arouse the antiforeign agitators, always ready to start trouble? Shuddering I recalled the riots of 1927, four years ago, the posters, "Down with Imperialists!" The fires that had burned several of the Christian school buildings and driven many foreigners from China. An "incident" now could break loose again into something much worse than our own personal lives and safety.

There must not be murder. There must not be false accusations. Where could I get help? Longing for Ralph, I watched with mounting dread the sunrise reflecting pearl yellow on the White Pagoda.

In the morning, I looked in on the sleeping Su-sieng. Giving Ka-trine her breakfast and doing the amah's chores, I tried to conceal the shaking of my hands, the sickness in my stomach.

Not trusting myself to look at Ne-dee, I instructed the cook to tell him to carry water from the well to fill to the brim all our large water jars. Then I saw the cook leave with his basket for market. Over and over the question repeated itself, "What shall I do?" I felt the moments running out.

I saw Ne-dee slopping his bucket of water into the large clay jar outside the kitchen…now Ai-nuk would be more bitter than ever. She would hate me—with reason. Why had we ever come to China?

As my shaking hands shifted the cans on the stubborn smoking coals a thought struck me—a mediator—a *go-between*—that's how the Chinese work. Talk price… neither side must lose face. To kill the boy would solve nothing. But a settlement for Ai-nuk…and, of course, our hospital for the child.

Whom could I find? My mind searched the list of our Chinese friends. Most were away for the extended vacation.

Lee Musu, I thought. Lee Musu, minister of the city church, recently back from his studies in America—I could talk with him. A Chinese, he would know how to mediate. Then I hesitated. *He is so young…and a scholar.* Would strong village men in a rage listen to him? Was it asking too much?

There seemed no alternative. With dry throat and awkward fingers, I fed Ka-trine. I listened at the amah's door and was grateful that Su-sieng still slept. Then leaving Ka-trine next door, I unlocked the gate by our garden and ran down the long flight of stone steps, across the deserted college yard, and up a narrow lane to a small Chinese house. To my intense relief Lee Musu answered my knock. Hurriedly I told my story. Trying to read his thoughts, I saw his sensitive face harden, his eyes fill with anger. I thought, *I am a foreigner and he is Chinese. This is a land where life is very cheap. Perhaps I have no right to ask him.*

He rose, his face a mask. Was he blaming me for what happened? Did he, too, think that one of our men was responsible? I could not believe it. But I felt shut out—alone.

But his voice was gentle as he said, "Go home now. I'll come and watch for the amah and her men from your neighbor's house. And when they come—you stay out of it, please."

Returning to my home, I knew it wasn't as simple as he made it sound. I had asked a Chinese to risk his life…I…a foreigner.

My apprehension mounted as the lonely morning dragged and the clock hands turned toward noon. Tensely I listened for the creaking of the college gate and Lee Musu—and watched the lower compound for the approach of Ai-nuk's family.

Once, hearing Su-sieng call out, I slipped into her room with another sleeping pill.

It was after twelve o'clock when I heard the college gate open and saw Lee Musu in his long blue Chinese coat, so slender and young, hurrying into the house across the walk from where he could watch for the amah's relatives.

In my own house, all was quiet. Ne-dee was below ironing, the cook working in the servants' downstairs kitchen. For me, terror filled the silent rooms. I felt sick, dizzy.

It was about two o'clock when I saw them coming. Lee Musu saw them, too, for he hurried over and concealed himself inside our house by the stairs that led down to the servants' quarters. Three sturdy men in coarse cotton short-coats and trousers climbed the hill toward our house. They were grimly silent. Ai-nuk, following, was pale.

I thought, *Now it will happen*. I wanted to run out and stop the men...but I could not. *You stay out of it, please*. They disappeared down the outer stone steps to the laundry below. I listened.

It came...all at once...Lee Musu running down the inside stairs...a cry...angry shouts...a struggle. I heard Lee Musu's explosive command, "Let go!" Silence. Lee Musu again, "Stop...let the boy go!"

Then the torrent of angry Chinese curses, Ai-nuk's high wail. Above the noise came Lee Musu's voice, sharp and icy cold. "Listen to me..." I felt the sudden silence. I heard his Chinese words, biting as a knife: "Trouble for you if you kill him... We must be sure first... Let him go now... Let's talk..."

I heard the men muttering, and the cook raising his voice in denial, and defense of the boy; then suddenly Ai-nuk crying out, "Look! Look at him—Ne-dee. He destroyed my child. He admits it!" There was the sound of a scuffle.

Lee Musu shouted, "Let go of him. Quiet, everyone... Trouble... Yes... What good to add murder...that will not help the girl. More trouble for all of you... Let's talk first..."

The voices, like dissonant chords, rose in high crescendo and modulated again...and again. The boy sobbed.

I went to my room and sat on my bed. The long process of Chinese mediation had begun…murder had been averted. But the longer process of restitution lay ahead—if restitution there could be.

This thing happened in our house!

It was mid afternoon when Lee Musu called me to come downstairs. He looked depleted and grim. "Your cook will take Ne-dee to their village now. We will watch him pack his things. Later we will try to find a way to help him."

At the foot of the stairs I looked into the boy's room—the narrow rattan bed, the crude one-drawer table and a wooden stool. Ne-dee, thin as he was, seemed to have shrunk, his sullen face drawn with fear. He rolled his ragged bed-quilt, his fingers shaking as they tried to tie the string around it. He couldn't have been over fifteen. He took down from a hook his one change of drab cotton trousers and jacket. From the drawer he brought out a broken comb and a set of dice. He glanced around the room. On the wall was a picture of mountains and a blue lake that I recognized as being from an American calendar Ralph had thrown out.

Ne-dee looked at it, then at me, his eyes defiant. "This is mine," he said.

I nodded and watched him fold it and put it in his pocket.

"Is that all?" Lee Musu asked.

Ne-dee looked around again and shrugged.

"You may go then."

The cook strode angrily ahead up the back garden steps. Ne-dee followed, his thin shoulders slumping, his eyes cast down.

The amah's three relatives had withdrawn to the garden, their faces impassive.

Lee Musu said, "I've persuaded Ai-nuk to take Su-sieng to the hospital. Her uncle will carry her. We'll all go down together."

So with the sleepy child in the arms of one of the men, we made a quiet procession down the walk and out the gate to the hospital. Ai-nuk wept. I was unable to comfort her.

Seeing the question in my eyes, Lee Musu continued, "They've agreed on a substantial settlement which the cook's family will pay the amah over a period of time. This will assure the girl's education. I have the cook's signature and the boy's thumb mark." He showed me a page torn from the cook's account book covered with Chinese characters, and a round ink smudge.

I said, "Tell Ai-nuk we'll pay the hospital expense."

"Of course." As a bridge between East and West, Lee Musu must have sensed what I was feeling. His eyes were kind now, forgiving me. "Give it time. Now rest your heart. You are not to blame."

But I could not let it go at that. Nor could Ai-nuk. There was no peace…my heart did not rest…and I was not at home in China. Through the coming months, with no excuse, she would strike back at me with sudden sharp words…as I sat at my desk…as I nursed my son Whitney.

She continued to "eat bitterness." She would say, "You come to China...you call yourselves Christians...but look what your people have done to my country...look what has happened to me..."

I understood her loneliness, resentment over her husband's death, the hurt of her child. But with my limited language, I could not argue or defend.

Time and again I was on the point of dismissing the unhappy woman. But she was always gentle with Ka-trine and Whitney. Moreover, trained amahs were almost impossible to find in these days of antiforeign propaganda. *Someday*, I thought stubbornly, *I will be able to convince her...to do something...* In the meantime I bought dresses for Su-sieng who had recovered and returned to school.

So Ai-nuk had been with us for two years, and I had not found the answer to my strained relations with her.

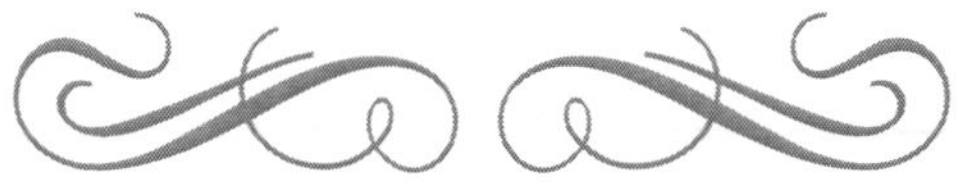

The Party

September 1931

Then came September 4, Ka-trine's third birthday. The air was still that morning, and I listened with particular attention to the sounds drifting up from the Chinese street that encircled our compound. My ears, sharply aware of danger signals, caught nothing ominous: only the usual strident horns of rickshaws, a vendor calling his bean-curd cakes, from the hill behind the White Pagoda a low slow thrum of the huge prayer gong.

I listened carefully—no gunfire—no shouts of demonstrators. Surely it was a good day—an auspicious day—to take Ka-trine to the fall party for the Chinese kindergartners. The Chinese teachers had urged us to come, and Ka-trine had been dancing her wide-eyed excitement, "Going to a party…a party!"

So when Ai-nuk said to me in her sharpest voice, "I think you should not take Ka-trine into the city streets today," it startled me…but I would not heed her warning.

Ai-nuk—Precious Jade—I watched her supple fingers linger on each button, ribbon, and bow of my child's party dress. *Why*, I wondered, *must she still be fighting me?* I had never been able to convince her that I wanted to be her friend, and on this hot morning, I was tired of trying. We had been looking forward to this party for days.

Giving Ka-trine one last loving brush of her hand, she turned to me, "I think you should not take her."

"I heard you, Ai-nuk. Why not?"

Her face grew tight, closing me out again. "There's trouble."

"There's always trouble."

The amah's eyes flashed. "You, you know nothing of trouble!"

"Oh, Ai-nuk, you've been saying these things for years. She'll have a good time at the party." Tired of this hostility between us, I continued, "Are you afraid to go? Is that why you speak of trouble?" Unfairly I moved up and taking my child's hand out of hers, said, "We're going."

With typical Chinese resignation, she shrugged. "If you must go, I'll go with you." She laid a conciliatory hand on Ka-trine's head, but her parting glance at me as she left the room was very clear, *I go for her sake, not yours.*

Something is defeating me, I thought. *Is it China… or Ai-nuk…or me?* Here was Ai-nuk, the part of China closest to me, defeating me each day. I had given her a good home and a job, and tried to prove that we weren't all "Foreign Devils"—or even "Long Noses"—that century-old epithet the Chinese had bestowed on the foreign barbarians whose noses "stuck out like the prows of their ships." What more could I do?

In a few moments, she returned in starched blue jacket and trousers, her jet black hair shining in a low coil into which she had tucked a fragrant jasmine blossom. Slender as a Chinese poem. She could be so pretty—when she smiled. I wanted to tell her so, but sighed as she darted me a resentful look. Now she would get even with me—she would go, but would be silent all the way.

We went down winding stone steps between ivy-covered buildings across the college yard where uniformed students passed us with friendly nods. Ka-trine, grasping Ai-nuk's hand, jumped happily along the sun-hot flagstones. Moving through the gate and along a deserted lane between high walls, I tried to walk beside them, but the amah pointedly dropped behind with my child, as custom decreed. For a short block and a few long moments, we walked this way, in silence…

Our lane ended at a narrow street that was jammed with honking rickshaws, bare-legged pullers, grunting load-bearers—a frightening tangle of noisy people and creaking wheels.

I hesitated. By now I wished I'd taken her advice—this was not a place for my child, too heavy for either of us to carry.

Stubbornly I pushed ahead, forcing a way among swaying baskets of vendors and the bargain seekers who dodged and elbowed in front of shops. Glancing back I saw right behind me Ka-trine holding to Ai-nuk and gazing wide-eyed into the food stalls where customers shouted over bamboo trays of water chestnuts and bean sprouts, or savory smelling pork balls steaming in a cart. How out of place my little girl looked in her fluffy yellow dress—and how helpless in the crush of hurrying people and jerking rickshaws. Once more I glanced back to the amah and my child.

"Come on…*come on*!"

But Ka-trine was not to be hurried. "Look! Look!" She pointed to a row of dried, pressed ducks hanging in a shop.

"Come on!" Reaching back for her hand and holding it tight, I started to cross an intersection. Then I stopped. Coming toward us, four coolies pulling a cart of crushed rock strained at the ropes and shouted at the traffic in their way. Passing in front of them trotted six sturdy men, their muscles bulging, as heavy loads of rice swayed from their shoulder poles.

"Make way…make way…" they chanted in counter-point.

But no one made way and the traffic snarled in a frenzy of Chinese oaths. We had to wait. The impatient crowd pressed close. Completely surrounded I felt utterly alone—and trapped. Tightening my hold on Ka-trine I thought, *How will I ever get her out of this unharmed?*

We had stopped in front of a shop with native oranges and tangerines piled before it in neat pyramids—a good retreat, I thought, and was about to duck into the stall when a Chinese girl with teasing black eyes suddenly spied us and leaped toward us from the shop. Her black braids tied with red string gleamed in the hot sun. Placing her hands on her blue trousered knees, her face close to my small daughter's, she screwed up her nose and laughed aloud then whirled around, braids swinging, and shrilled to the street, "*Huang-guay…Dong-pay!* Foreign Devil…Long Nose!"

She turned back for another prolonged stare. "Little foreign child—how funny she looks!" Glancing about she shouted, "Come see…*Huang-guay…Dong-pay!*"

Shielding Ka-trine, I forced myself to smile at the girl, but she ignored me. "Ai-nuk!" I called over my shoulder. She did not answer.

A dozen curious boys and girls jumped out from the nearby shops, their eyes sparkling. Two barefoot boys in patched shorts ducked in front of the impatient cart pullers and joined us. The first girl squealed, "Look at her funny nose!" Soon one shrill voice and then another took up the century old cry, "Long Nose…Foreign Devil!"

Then it became a chorus. Braids bobbed as the children jumped and pointed, chanting, "*Huang-guay… Dong-pay*!"

Ka-trine stared as they danced wildly around her.

"Ai-nuk!" For a moment my eyes left my child to search for the amah. I couldn't see her.

I had been in such crowds before, unafraid because I knew they were merely curious about me. But now it was different—my child was being threatened. I felt her hands clinging to my skirt. Her eyes were wide… pleading…

"Ai-nuk!" I called again. Above the noise, I heard Ka-trine's muffled echo, "Ai-nuk!" I wanted to weep.

The crowd, blocking all traffic, now filled the street. In near panic I saw again the cartload of crushed rock and heard the shouts of the pullers. A boy's taunting scream broke into my mounting fears.

"Look at the little *Huang-guay*!"

"No, not *Huang-guay*, friends!" I held out my hands. "Friends!"

Not heeding me the children grew bolder. A girl's grubby fingers reached out to feel Ka-trine's light dress, so different from her course blue trousers and jacket. Another, giggling, touched my child's brown hair. The girl with the red string on her braids put an excited finger on Ka-trine's small nose crying, "Look!" and laughed shrilly, while the rest, menacing now, or so it seemed to me, shouted, "*Huang-guay*!"

My child hid her face in my skirt.

Behind the children, jostling Chinese men and women peered over shoulders to see the cause of the commotion. Wildly my eyes tried to pierce the crowd. Bitterly I thought, *Ai-nuk's doing this to get even with me—she's deserted us.*

I glanced down. Ka-trine leaned against me and sobbed, "Ai-nuk!"

I took up her cry, "Ai-nuk…Ai-nuk! Help us!"

Then I saw her hiding in the crowd. As if waiting to hear just this, she came. She was no longer small and smoldering—she had suddenly grown tall—her eyes alive now like hot coals, flashing. Facing the children, shaking a finger at them, she shouted above their voices, "Be quiet! Be quiet!"

The children recognizing her as one of their own were miraculously silent. They stopped smiling. Swinging around the circle and pointing her finger the amah cried, "Stupid ones, listen to me. Where are your manners? Who taught you? Are you children of devils?"

The children, drawing away, looked fearfully at one another. The amah now pointed at herself. "Look at *me*. Are you listening?

The boys and girls stared at Ai-nuk's flushed face and gesticulating hand. Now she lowered her voice coaxing them in the wily manner of the great story-teller.

"Come here…I'll tell you a story. A true story. Listen…I know this small girl. How? You don't believe me? I'll tell you. I came to her when she was born. I've watched over her and fed her. Do you hear? Come close."

They watched cautiously, pushing closer to the amah.

"You called her '*Huang-guay*.' This little 'Foreign Devil' is just like you. You don't believe me? I tell you, when she is hungry, she wants food…just like you. When she is thirsty, she drinks…like you. And her nose…" Ai-nuk bent over and touched my child's nose lovingly, "her nose is like yours…all the same as yours. When the cake is good, she smells it…*ai-haaa*! When she is happy, she laughs. And when she is hurt, she cries…"

The amah pointed to the sobbing Ka-trine. "Now… look now—what you have done! Now…what do you think? Are you Chinese devils…or aren't you?"

The whole street watched as the children gazed at Ka-trine, a slow wonder lighting their faces. Then the fruit merchant's daughter, her eyes on the amah's face, backed step by step to the shop, and from the golden pyramid reached for a tangerine. She brought it and stooping held it out to Ka-trine.

"Take!"

My little one buried her face in my skirt. Then as the older child spoke softly to her, Ka-trine turned and slowly...slowly reached out for the tangerine. As she felt its orange skin, she smiled.

This was the cue. Every child darted to the fruit and snatching a piece brought it to the little *Huang-guay*. The merchant's girl took hold of Ka-trine's short skirt making it a basket, and the children dropped their fruit into it, laughing as they scrambled for some tangerines that rolled on the cobbles. Ka-trine laughed with them. I thought, how quickly the wind changes!

Beyond the children the shop owner stood, arms folded, staring at us—then I saw his black cap—nodding as he smiled at Ka-trine. And putting his hands into his wide sleeves, he bowed to me. The tangerines were his gift.

A policeman's shrill whistle startled the watching crowd. Children ducked. Adults pushed on about their business. The policeman, beckoning to us, opened a way across the intersection.

As we moved along I heard the children's shrill voices, "Come back and play, *Huang-guay*!" I waved.

We turned into a quiet lane, Ai-nuk walking proudly, her head high. Between us trotted Ka-trine chuckling over her skirt full of tangerines. I wiped my forehead and my knees stopped trembling. The amah was murmuring, "The stupids…the little stupids!"

Simultaneously we glanced back and saw the cart with its load of crushed rock rolling past the intersection. I wanted to say something, but could not find the right Chinese words—I could only reach out and touch Ai-nuk's hand. Her rigid face was gentle now.

Brushing her hand softly over my little girl's head, she laughed softly. "*Huang-guay?*" She smiled into my eyes with a light that reached out and embraced the three of us. I saw the white jasmine shining in her hair… and suddenly I was aware that at last she was walking beside me!

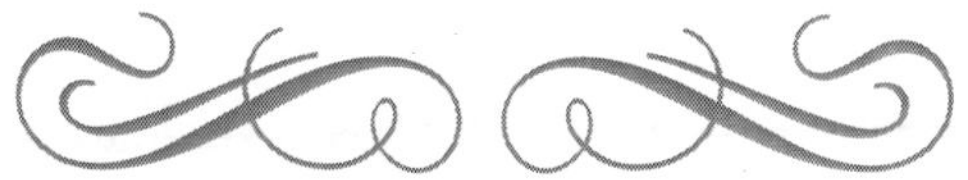

Hope Can Warm a Man

Winter 1931

I didn't see how we could possible celebrate Christmas in our home or with our students at Foochow College that Winter of 1931. Then unexpectedly, three students came to our house, bowed, which was surprising, and made a startling request.

"Choi Sinang (Shrader Teacher), we would like to be the three kings in the Christmas pageant this year."

Amazed, my husband gazed intently at the solemn-eyed seniors. "Why do you want this?" These boys were leaders, sometimes for good, sometimes trouble.

The Christmas pageant, presented by the students, was given twice, once for the schools as a dress rehearsal, and again for outsiders. It attracted people of all ranks from that ancient Chinese city.

Ru-fu grinned and swept back the lock of long black hair that fell over his forehead. "We have a reason. We can't tell it now. But we promise we will be hot-hearted to carry the pageant."

Dai-hok added, "We'll make students come to rehearsals on time and behave. Even Go-ming."

Ralph laughed. "Go-ming."

Ming-sing said, "Always you teachers have given the Christmas party for us. This time we students have a plan—a surprise for you."

When Ralph finally consented, I could see he was pleased, but with reservations.

Ru-fu, Dai-hok, and Ming-sing were more than actors. They were scriptwriters and directors at the Saturday afternoon rehearsals. They saw that the students came promptly and cooperated. They translated the Christmas story into the Foochow dialect. With Ming-sing's inspired imagination, they plotted astonishing scenes we never would have thought of.

I was put in charge of costumes. Dismayed with the bedraggled crowns and faded draperies I found in the school auditorium closet, I turned to the boys. They shook their heads. "Come with us."

They led me through narrow streets to the theatrical guild shops of secondhand costumes. Ming-sing pointed to a rack. "Ha, that is what we want." The shopkeeper pulled out some old stage costumes with glinting threads of gold-etched dragons on crimson satin, and other oriental splendors. They could be mended. He led us to a dusty chest filled with high headdresses sparkling with jewels in the style of the old theater.

Dai-hok, always clowning, spotted a leopard skin, stiff and smelly. I shuddered, but he said, "For Go-ming. He can frighten the goat herds."

The weeks passed with classes and pageant preparations. Rehearsals became exciting. The boys, natural actors, became the people of the play and improvised. Sometimes they got carried away—especially Go-ming with his leopard skin.

During the pageant preparations, whenever we appeared unexpectedly among the students, they would break off their conversations. But I had little time to wonder.

I was busy, too, and one day when Ralph said to me. "Let's take a walk," I was preoccupied until he added, "I have something to show you. Up there." I glanced toward the low hill that rose just outside our college compound. From our house we could see the cluster of Chinese temples silhouetted against the sky. This November afternoon they looked cold. Reluctantly I grabbed a coat. Soon we let ourselves out through the squeaky wooden side gate. Moving along a narrow lane between walls, we skirted the White Pagoda compound and climbed the uneven stone steps of the rocky hill. Ralph led the way. Shivering, I tried to keep up. At the top, we passed the deserted Taoist temple and the Buddhist temple where a solitary yellow-robed priest shuffled across an empty court to beat a gong.

Clutching our coats against the cold north wind, we rounded a wall and looked ahead. I stood rooted. Instead of the usual bare hillside, I saw a city of straw huts, shoulder high, roofs rounded like sampans. Hundreds of these mat sheds stretched across the hill and down. Between the rows of huts, several men and women in threadbare garments were building open fires with weeds. "They're flood victims," Ralph said. "The government has transported them down the coast in ships and dumped them on the cities, hoping they won't freeze to death till they can get back to their lands in the spring. There are about a thousand on this hill, and thousands elsewhere."

Appalled, I asked, "What will happen to them?"

"A few will pull rickshaws. I'm told that those who can't get jobs will join the soldiers or the bandits, or go upriver to join the Communists. In the spring they'll go back north—those that survive."

I watched a woman feed dried grass into her little fire, shielding it with her frayed coat. She called to two children tugging at stubborn weeds with cold-reddened hands. Though I couldn't speak their dialect, I understood. "Hurry," she screamed.

"We can't pull them," cried the boy.

Ralph ran to the children and tugged at the weeds till they came loose. "Here," he said.

A tall man with long sparse whiskers approached us, his hands hugging themselves in his wide sleeves. He bowed to each of us. "My name, Soong, Lau Soong," he said. *Old Soong*, I thought and guessed he was their leader. After a few stumbling words, we left.

Ralph and I had to concentrate on our classes at the college and on rehearsals for the pageant. It seemed like irrelevant playacting against the stark reality of the hill, and many nights I heard the wind and fancied it finding every hole in the flimsy rattan sheds. The older church leaders, American and Chinese, organized to gather supplies, find jobs, start a day nursery. But it was all so little. I felt helpless.

At last it was December 23—the night of the real performance for the city people. My hands shook as I fastened in place the glass-jeweled headdress of Ru-fu, the first king, whose eyes were as bright as jewels. Running down the winding steps from the college auditorium to the church below, I felt the excitement of the costumed students swarming in the courtyard. All was ready now, so I pushed through the crowd and entered the side door.

The large unheated sanctuary was filling rapidly, the Chinese women going to the stiff red-lacquered benches on the left, the men on the right. How cold it was! Crowding into a seat about halfway down, I sat beside a Chinese woman carrying a hot charcoal brazier. A little warmth might creep out to my chilled fingers and toes.

Glancing at the platform, I marveled at the ingenuity of our students. They had transformed the bare walls across the front of the church. Feathery bamboo trees framed the nativity scene hidden behind screens. The shed's curving roof and flowing lines of the trees made a Chinese painting. Above this, a long scroll of crimson and gold proclaimed in Chinese characters, "I Came That They May Have Life."

The balconies filled with the blue-robed choirs from the girls' school. Near me, women took children onto their laps, making room for newcomers. Yet most of the front rows were roped off. For whom? Some high officials?

In the air of expectancy, I almost forgot that a war was going on around Shanghai, where bombs had been falling, and that an enemy gunboat lay anchored in our river, its guns trained on our city. Whatever lay ahead, tonight the universal hope for peace would be enacted on our stage and claim our hearts.

About me were clean, hard-working men and women. Were they yearning for something to give them hope—for peace, for a world without bombs, without fear? To some it would be the first time they had heard the Christmas story. Would its deeper meaning reach them? Or was it just too foreign?

Suddenly there was a commotion at the rear of the church. Through the wide doors came a crowd of men and women in the threadbare padded garments of the North—the refugees from the hill. Reluctantly, as if pushed on by others, they moved forward and were ushered by students into the front rows. Then I saw the tall man, Old Soong with his long whiskers. The young Chinese minister, Lee Musu, was bowing him to a seat in the front row.

Why hadn't I thought of the party the students had mentioned? This was their surprise!

A too-thin woman was urged into a seat. When she saw me, her face filled with terror. She sat down on the edge of the bench as if ready to run for the door. In dismay I thought, *They are afraid of us. They can't understand our dialect. They'll be noisy and won't comprehend. What will happen to our pageant?*

Music filled the church, "O Come, All Ye Faithful." We stood, reaching for the small blue books, traced with our fingers the rows of Chinese characters, and sang in Chinese, slightly off-key, "joyful and triumphant…"

The hymn ended; the student procession started. Everybody looked back. The clashing cymbals—how right they were! Like all the street processions.

The flute players piped their shrill Chinese tunes. Students dressed as beggars shook coppers in their begging bowls. Goatherds in gunnysack coats shuffled their straw sandals and tugged a live goat, which stopped to bleat and shake its stubborn head. Go-ming in his leopard skin pranced behind, nudging the goat and bringing shouts from the children. Farmers came with baskets of tangerines, papayas, sugared dates. Ten students made up as coolies staggered under heavy bags of rice, groaned and mopped their brows. King Herod strutted with his armed guard.

Finally came the three kings, Ru-fu, Dai-hok, and Ming-sing, solemn in their oriental robes.

At the front of the church, the actors placed their gifts on a table and disappeared behind the screens. Lee Musu moved to the platform. Could he catch the attention of that restless audience? Especially those from the hill?

Pointing to the crimson scroll, he said, "Life for whom? Listen!" He spoke in the Northern tongue. Surprised, the men and women from the north stopped talking. Was all this a trick?

"The story you are about to see is filled with such truth that around the world people of every race are celebrating it tonight. Peasants and scholars, poor men and kings, come to worship the God *who cares*—who cares for *all* men—even men driven by flood to a cold hill. He is the God who sent His Son to teach men the way to peace. He works through men. He worked through the hearts of these students who prepared this celebration for you."

The cymbals clashed. The house lights dimmed. Revealed in the circle of shifting spotlights, a child was leading a docile leopard. A voice spoke of swords and plows. Then came a familiar village scene.

"Ai-ha," murmured the audience, as angry tax collectors tore baskets of grain from the farmers' hands. *"Ai-ha, ai-ha,"* they cried when soldiers burst in. Later, when a leopard jumped out, frightening the goatherds, they discovered it was only a playful goat-boy in disguise, teasing the others. How they laughed!

I began to relax. *This is real*, I thought. *How well our students knew!*

At last it was the night of the Star—the cowering goatherds, the angels' song.

Be not afraid…

The screens parted. A Chinese Mary and Joseph leaned over the babe, and worshipers presented their gifts.

"Silent night…" Softly the Chinese word of the choirs filled the church.

"Hush." Mothers leaned over their children. "Shh… hush…hush…"

Peace on earth! Listen, their yearning faces said. *God cares for all men. Someday they will not hate—drop bombs. Someday we will know we are all God's children.*

The three kings came—Ru-fu, Dai-hok, and Ming-sing. They placed their crowns before the manger and bowed low. The light dimmed on the manger scene.

I sat in blackness. All about me the breathless silence cried, *What will happen now to the little King—the one who brings peace and love? Heaven help the little King!*

A clash of cymbals sent a shiver through me. I heard the tread of soldiers' marching feet. Ominous. Nearer. The hunt was on for the new little King that threatened Herod's power. On the darkened stage soldiers shouted, swords hammered on a door. A woman cried out. Silence came again, and silence of a thousand hearts. The soldiers' tramping steps receded.

Has the hope of the world been destroyed?

A pause hung in the blackness.

But look—a light—dim, then brighter. It shone on Joseph and Mary, safe in a distant land. And the babe. They have escaped. Ah, the little King. He lives....

Like a single breath a sigh swept the audience.

"Joy to the world," the choirs sang out. "Let earth receive her King!"

The houselights came on, and Ru-fu stood on the platform. "To you, our guests from the North, I speak. When we walked on your hill and heard your story, our hearts were very hot for you. We students cannot change our country's bad condition in a hurry, but someday we will make a better China so people will not suffer as you are doing.

"Tonight we wish to make the Christian Festival of Giving with you. Our gifts are too small. But they are the symbol of God's love. Come now to receive them."

The procession down the aisles was no make-believe. The patched garments were not costumes. The hunger-hollow cheeks, the sores on a child's head, were not painted on. The man limping with a crude crutch was not play-acting.

Each head of family carried a slip of paper and received from the students at the table large bags of rice according to the number in his family. The children came to receive the tangerines, vegetables, and sugarcane. They ran back to their places laughing.

When the last gift was received, Old Soong bowed from the waist to Ru-fu. Turning, he faced us, and pointed to the crimson scroll. "What you say is true," his strong old voice rang out. "For such a king we have longed. *Until* today have been dying. *From* today we shall live!"

He motioned to his people, and they rose to follow him to the straw huts on the hill.

Later, as the boys joined us by our fireside, Ralph asked, "How did you do it?"

Ru-fu answered, "After you took us up the hill to see the refugees, we told the other students they had to go, a few at a time, and see for themselves. One evening, the refugees thought two boys were spying on them and started to throw stones."

Ming-sing picked up the story. "The boys ran—all the way down the hill. They told us we shouldn't have made them go. So we went up and found their leader, Old Soong, and explained."

Ru-fu said, "We saw the look in his eyes—so sad and yet so proud. On the way down, we decided on the Christmas party for them. We would get all the students to buy rice."

Dai-hok, the roguish one, interrupted. "Some said, 'Why should we give money for people who don't belong to our families? We're not responsible for them.' We told them they had to go and see, or they couldn't be in the pageant."

"Some of the boys don't have much money, you know," said Ming-sing. "But after they went up and talked with the people, they wanted to give something, if only a few tangerines. Some gave enough to buy the big bags of rice."

Dai-hok explained, "The hardest one to get was our fat school cook." Finally we made him walk up the hill. How he grumbled! He said, "All-light. I'll hold back half the rice I cook for you till the foreign festival, including my share. *For them.* And if your bellies grumble, you'll know better how they feel on that hill."

Ru-fu pushed back his troublesome lock of hair and looked directly at Ralph. "Did you see the people's eyes when they came to get their rice tonight? Most were pleased. But some were still angry."

Ralph said, "If you'd lost your homes and been hungry for months, might not you be angry too?

Ru-fu nodded. "It's cold in those huts on the hill. But perhaps they won't feel the cold so much tonight. The rice wasn't all we gave them. Hope can warm a man."

"Choi Sinang, sometimes it is the Communists who teach us. We want to help our country. How can we know which way is best?"

The light of the fire flickered. Ralph got up and poked the flame. It flared up, casting shadows on the thoughtful faces. Ralph's was hidden from me, but his words came vibrantly, "Which of your sages remarked, 'Teachers open doors…pupils must enter by themselves'?"

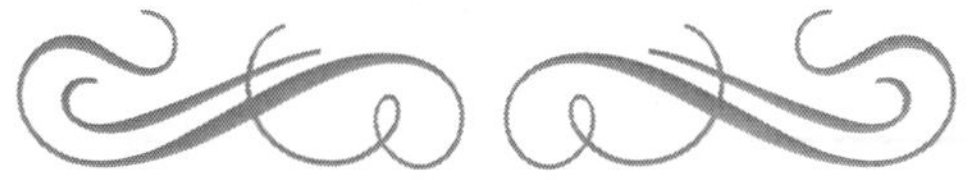

Shou Hsing Gung

(Old Star Grandfather)

June 1932

Suddenly it was our last week, and we were packing to go home. That June morning Ru-fu came to the house, and as I opened the door to him, I saw distress in his eyes.

"Please, Sinaniong, I must speak to Sinang."

"He's down at the college. But come in."

When I saw the frown deepen on Ru-fu's face, my heart went out to this tall poised student, president of the senior class. Now he looked hot and unhappy. That lock of black hair that he used to toss around the first two years when he was arrogant and antiforeign had fallen again over his forehead. He pushed it back.

"What's wrong?"

He started to speak and stopped. Then in one breath, "Sinaniong, I hate to say…but feast must be postponed."

"Oh, Ru-fu, not again!"

This was the second postponement of the farewell feast our senior students had arranged for us at Foochow's famous Seven Bamboo Restaurant, and which we had been anticipating beyond reason.

"Very sorry. Class is sorry. Restaurant is sorry—I have just come from there—but will do, a week from tonight. Can you come then?"

"It's our last night in Foochow." I hesitated. "We leave the next morning. I don't know."

He looked embarrassed. "I can't explain reason now. Very important reason—very troublesome. Later on you know. We all lose much face. You see, this very big occasion. It is circumstance beyond control makes change necessary." Tiny beads of sweat stood on his forehead.

I couldn't stand the distress in his eyes. Glancing at the half-filled trunks trailing from our bedroom into the wide hall, and thinking of the full week ahead, I felt dismay at the postponement, but relief that the feast was not cancelled.

"Tell the boys of course we'll come. Tell them not to be troubled."

The grateful smile he gave me now as he wiped his forehead and left was enough reward for my decision.

But with growing uneasiness I returned to the jumble of clothes, linens, shoes, Chinese curios—the accumulation of six years that refused to sort itself into what to leave and what to take. A pile of examination papers stared at me from my desk.

Why, I wondered, did they have to do this? The invitation given us so enthusiastically by the officers of the class weeks ago had been the brightest spot in those hectic days. The students had invited us because they wanted to, and refused to take no for an answer. This, after all the upheavals and hostility, had warmed us, and helped cancel out my other feeling—can we get away before something explodes?

As I wrapped a blanket around a Ching bowl, a thought hit me hard, draining the strength from my knees. Deserting the packing, I went to the porch and dropped on the step. That must be the reason. It was the same old wall—we were white! We were foreigners! Symbols of the West. We could never be really accepted in these troubled times.

The class must have split—right down the middle, as it had repeatedly in the past. Gau-daik and his followers, influenced by antiforeign agitators, must be boycotting the feast for the American teachers. My throat was dry as I sat, head in hands. Except for the loyal Ru-fu, Dai-hok, Ming-sing and a few more, the others were still hostile, and Ru-fu was trying for time to persuade them.

I shuddered, recalling the antiforeign demonstrations, the two college buildings that had been burned, the student strikes. This we understood—these passionate yearnings of a proud people to be free of the West. I thought, too, of the two armies approaching Foochow from the south and the west—the armies that caused our years in China to be cut short. And no one knew how many Communist sympathizers were concealed in our city, or our school.

If some of our students were still bitter to Ralph and me as individuals, seeing only our white skins, what had our six years accomplished? Nothing? After all the work, the long night hours, the listening? Nothing! We had friends among the boys, but what of the troublemakers? Behind their reserved faces, did they still hate us? Do we leave them anything—anything at all? I could have had my children anywhere, but what about Ralph? Was it worth the best years of his life to try to prove we weren't all imperialists? At this point it would take a miracle to convince me of any value in our coming to China.

As I shoved myself to my feet, my eyes rested for a moment on the seven-storied White Pagoda beyond our wall. A thousand years old, the scholars said. Ten hundred years! Pointing its curved roof to heaven, patiently it brooded over my small impatience. What were six years?

Comforted to a degree, I went indoors to my packing, but still full of questions. What is Ru-fu really thinking? What is wrong with our students, and the feast?

Our final week passed in a tangle of emotions, of meetings, of uncompleted tasks, while the real threats of armies and uprisings kept upsetting my efforts to be calm. Yet when friends came holding out red wrapped gifts, I thought—*how can we leave these people?*

Late one evening Ralph pushed down the lids of the two large trunks. They would not close. So climbing on them he jumped, while I, sweating, struggled with the clasps till at last they snapped into place.

"Finished," said Ralph. "Now, not another thing. We can't take another thing."

I glanced at a large closed suitcase and the still open wardrobe trunk surrounded by piles of essentials. "Except those."

As I pushed a pair of Ralph's tennis shoes into the bottom of the wardrobe trunk, I saw that even Ralph's strong shoulders were drooping.

Then the front door knocker sounded.

Smiling boys from the junior class were holding out a bulky package in red rice paper. "Wrap off paper. See if you like…." Did we like! The set of black lacquer trays was bright with gold dragons, phoenix, coins, and butterflies. "And see—your name in Chinese—Choi Ung-daik—Man on Mountain!"

From the huge suitcase, Ralph pulled out his old college football sweater—and in went the trays.

The girls' school sent a glowing young Chinese teacher.

"Here, from junior and senior girls—the ones you met with to discuss modern-girl problems. They want you to have a new style Chinese dress—not loose and floppy like old one you have now." She helped me slip on the slender russet brocade slit to the knee. "Paris model." She laughed.

I rubbed my fingers over the rich silk. "Tell them my American friends will all want one like this!"

From the women's hospital the Chinese doctor came asking, "Where is your son?" I brought Whitney, my nineteen-month-old boy, and we laughed at his puzzled eyes as her skillful fingers slipped onto him the little blue long-coat she had made by hand, and black cap with red button on top. Hugging him, her bright eyes flashed. "To remind him Chinese doctor helped bring him into world."

The hand-wrought pewter teapot, engraved with a Chinese poem she also gave me, would recall my hours in the hospital teaching English medical terms to the nurses, and seeing through their eyes China's overwhelming physical needs.

One morning Ai-nuk, the amah, placed two red bowls and short red chopsticks before the children. "Now, eat rice every day with these—and in America don't forget *amah*!"

And Kong-dia, even Kong-dia, our ill-tempered house-boy, put a small tin of sweet smelling jasmine tea at my place, and when I thanked him, his glum face lighted for a moment.

So, day by day, the lovely dismaying gifts came, and Ralph and I touched them—for each one bore some facet of China's beauty—and loved them because they were so totally unexpected. And removing some useful article from the suitcase or the wardrobe trunk, we found a place for each one.

Throughout all this, all the week, the postponed feast hung, an uneasy backdrop, in my mind.

Then it was the last day. Even then we did not know what to expect at the Seven Bamboos—even when the trunks were closed, and the rickshaws jerked and jounced us through crowded South Street to the restaurant.

It was small comfort that ahead of us rode the solemn Ming-sing and round faced Dai-hok escorting us. Ru-fu was missing.

Climbing the narrow stairs of the restaurant to the private dining room above, I scarcely noticed the bowing waiter and the enticing smells of Chinese cooking. I expected Ru-fu to be waiting at the entrance. He was not there. *Who*, I kept asking, *who will be here…?*

We followed a narrow balcony overlooking the court to a wide door and stopped. My heart stopped—and then cried out—forgive my doubts!

The room was filled—filled with our senior students! When they saw us, they clapped and bowed and grinned all at once.

By the crinkles around Ralph's eyes, I knew how he was feeling.

The boys, their blue uniforms clean and pressed, surrounded us. Now I saw, to my delight, two other guests—two students who had graduated the year before. But Ru-fu?

I asked Ming-sing. "Oh, no trouble. No trouble. Ru-fu will come. Do not worry. We wait."

So we wait, I thought, now suddenly hungry. *But why?*

Ming-sing clapped for attention. "Please be seated in chairs around side of room. Please forgive slight delay."

Hungrier each minute, I waited with the others. Hungrier as we smelled the spicy smells and heard the shouts of the happy diners below. Impatiently we cracked salty toasted watermelon seeds with our teeth—and waited. The noise from below became louder, the smells more pungent, and we so hungry we could scarcely endure to wait.

The boys grew restless, whispering to each other. Their eyes kept glancing toward the door.

At length a barefoot waiter ran into the room crying in Chinese, "Go to the tables. Head cook says the food will get cold. You must eat now or all the expensive dishes he has made will be spoiled. All his hard work wasted. The reputation of the shop ruined. You must eat."

The boys jumped up. "Yes…eat!"

Ming-sing shrugged. "Come to the tables, then. We wait no more. Sorry for small delay."

I was still wondering about Ru-fu as we took our places at the round tables for ten. Small side dishes and a large steaming bowl were placed in the center of each table. Chinese lanterns lighted the sleek black hair of the students, the anticipation in their eyes. Impatiently they waited for Ming-sing to lift his chopsticks with the words, "Please eat." We all dipped at once into the bowls to pull out a piece of tender beef or mushroom or water chestnut covered with savory sauce.

At my right sat Ding-chung, guest, back from the University in Peking (Modern name Beijing). Observing the new maturity in his face, I remembered him as we first knew him—clown, magic-maker, flute player. And also our gardener, carrying our water up the hill in his buckets like a coolie, so he could remain in school. I recalled his letter from Peking: "I sleep on the porch…the colder it is outside the warmer in my bedding it is! I live in a palace like a king while all about me are suffering... But who will blame me if I do this to sharpen my tools so that I may one day help my people?"

In a pause between a main dish and a sweet bowl, Ding-chung stood and clapped for attention. Gracefully sweeping his magician hands he snatched from mid-air a scroll and read a testimonial in Chinese, which we couldn't understand. But there was no mistaking the shouts and applause.

Across the table was the other guest, Huo-hok, Happy Harmony. To our surprise he had endured the crowded launch trip up the river from Fukien University to be with us. I recalled his hot disposition, his bitter eyes of four years ago at the time of the fires. Had he really had a part in that? It was never proven. Seeing the open friendliness in his face now, I could not think so.

Through the meal, my eyes kept wandering to Ru-fu's empty place.

After the sixteen courses—the sweet-sour meat dishes, the pink slices of Peking duck, the whole fish grinning at us under his red-hot-pepper sauce—after the almond cakes, and finally after the hot steaming towels had been passed around, and it was almost time to go—just then we heard a commotion on the balcony, and Ru-fu, black hair awry, rushed into the room. Breathless, he was lugging a long, heavy wooden box. He flashed his quick smile. The boys cheered.

Placing the box on the floor, he said, "Please forgive. I am sorry for delay."

"Eat, now, Ru-fu…eat," the students called as waiters brought back bowls of food. Barely tasting it, Ru-fu answered in Chinese the questions they threw at him. Then turning to Ralph and wiping his forehead, he said, "*Ai-ha*, China is slow. Not fast like America—never on time!"

As his chopsticks probed the dishes, he said, "Now I can explain reason why we postpone feast, reason for delays. Students want to give you gift."

"But, Ru-fu, this feast is a great gift," I said.

"We want to give you gift to take to America—very best we can think of, but students have hard time to decide on gift. That is first delay. At last we decide and go to best craftsman in city, choose very best wood—must wait for finest wood to come—more delay. We say, no apprentice make this gift. Must be Master Craftsman himself. Master gets sick—more delay. We postpone dinner, once—*ai-ha*, twice! Lose face. Cause you much trouble. Master Craftsman promises us tonight gift will be ready. But no. When I arrive at restaurant, the gift is not here, so I go to shop. Still not ready. Teeth not ready."

Teeth! I wondered.

"Master Craftsman must put in teeth, and polish once more. Make perfect. Ahhh, that is China—all by hand—not fast like machines make in America. Someday China will be scientific, then make things fast!"

We watched Ru-fu, unable to speak.

"Now," he said, putting down his chopsticks, "now I make you my speech." Pushing back his hair, he bowed to us and spoke in Mandarin. The boys watched him, nodding their approval.

When the applause ended, Ralph, paraphrasing the Chinese courtesy terms in English said, "Please, Ru-fu, in your exalted land we are unworthy visitors, and speak poorly your language. We cannot understand the Mandarin tongue used by scholars like you. Would you translate into our miserable language, English?"

Miserable language! How the students laughed.

With unexpected frankness, Ru-fu said, "Choi Sinang, I speak truth. I used to think all Americans had ugly face, and their heart would be the same as their face. I thought if one day I had power I must destroy all their schools in China."

I saw a swift glance pass between him and Huo-hok.

"When my father bade me enter Foochow College to see if it was good or not, I learn that the foreigners at my school were very kind—their heart just opposite their not-well-looking faces. You teach us our Nationalism must be steppingstone to internationalism—so all countries work together for good of whole world." The students applauded. Ru-fu silenced them.

"You, Mr. Shrader, have been full of trouble by us. But sometimes late at night you listen to us, and search with us for purpose—for meaning of life. You teach us to question, and to find our answers—about Man, about what is freedom. You talk with us about Tao—the way.

The Lao-tzu way, the Buddha way, the Jesus way, the God way. Then we forget you are foreigner—you are Choi Ung-daik—Man on Mountain."

The boys did not stir. Ru-fu, glancing toward them, smiled. "Now our teachers leave us, and we are sad." He turned to us. "But we send with you our humble gift so you will never forget your unworthy students."

Ming-sing and Dai-hok set the long box upright on the table, lifted the lid, and Shou Hsing Gung stood before us. A breath of approval came from the boys who gathered around.

I gasped, seeing at first a grotesque figure. Looking more closely I saw an old man standing twenty inches tall and peering into my eyes. Carved from the root of a dark-wood tree, his shining head rose into a high dome. I saw how deep and expert the carving—how he glowed from every polished curve of his flowing robes, from the gnarled staff on which he leaned. Tiny ivory teeth showed in his laughing mouth, and the whites of his ivory eyes twinkled at us.

Ru-fu said, "Ming-sing, you are China scholar. Explain."

Ming-sing laid his long fingers on the polished head. "This is god of immortality. You see, he has high forehead. Denotes wisdom. He leans on staff—Staff of Long Life. He carries in left hand the Magic Peach."

Looking at Ralph and me, he said, "This Magic Peach comes from a tree beyond Western Mountains. Tree blossoms once in three thousand years, fruit ripens in another three thousand years. Taste this Peach—a man becomes immortal. Our gift is symbol to you—Old Star Grandfather is very best wish one friend can give another. Tonight by this gift, you taste Peach of Immortality. You receive wisdom. You give us Father Christmas. We give you Shou Hsing Gung!"

I scarcely noticed the Old Man. I saw instead the bright-eyed students about us. The faces blurred. Suddenly I knew a part of me would not leave China—ever.

Later that evening when Ralph and I climbed the hill of our compound, we stopped to gaze for the last time as the moon-bright leaves of the banyan tree and the White Pagoda turned to white jade. Then reluctantly we moved on to our house and entered the dimly lighted living room. Setting the heavy box on the floor, Ralph lifted the lid, then placed the carving on the table. Now, transformed in the magic mystery of the half-light, and our emotions of the evening, it was no longer a Thing—it was a *he*—a Person—winsomely teasing us. Silently we gazed at Old Star Grandfather, who smiling confidently back, said, "I have come to live with you."

This could happen, I marveled, even in a revolution. This was the miracle!

But as I rubbed my fingers over the satin wood of his shining head, I knew with a stab of realism he would have to be a lonely Old Man.

I shook my head. "We can't possibly take him."

Ralph sighed. "We can't *not* take him!"

Then, glancing at the hall full of closed trunks, he shook his head, too, and switched off the light.

During the remainder of that last tossing night, Shou Hsing Gung's winning smile had been at work, for next morning, in the confusion of children's and amah's tears, suitcases, and farewells, I ran into the living room, grabbed the Old Man, and carried him to the upright wardrobe trunk. Forcing it open, I pulled out the shoes and laid Shou Hsing Gung in a towel, behind my dresses, where he barely fit at a precarious angle. There was no time to tie him, but accommodatingly he remained in place as I pulled the two sides of the trunk together and fastened the lock.

Several stages of travel later—rickshaw, sampan, river launch, coastal steamer—on the ocean steamer between Hong Kong and Singapore, Ralph decided to open the trunk. As he pushed the sides apart the ship lunged, and out rolled a white-robed object. He stared, pulling off the towel, and stared again at Old Star Grandfather smiling triumphantly at him. I watched the two of them.

Poker-faced, rubbing his hand over Shou Hsing Gung's polished dome, Ralph said, "And where are my tennis shoes?"

I pointed to the bamboo basket beside our son's crib.

Ralph grinned. "But you said we couldn't possibly bring him." His eyes were as bright as Old Star Grandfather's. "Partner, I knew you'd find a way!"

In spite of the ship's rolling, I sighed happily as Ralph wrapped the man in his towel and returned him to his uncomfortable bed behind my skirts.

From Singapore to Switzerland, whenever we opened the trunk, Shou Hsing Gung tumbled out grinning roguishly, but in time we mastered the trick of holding him in his bed while closing the trunk.

❋ ❋ ❋

Through the years, wherever we have made our home, Old Star Grandfather has his special place on his own table in our living room. Through the years, as happens to many of us, he seems to lean more heavily on his staff. His ivory teeth have fallen out, and his eyes are not quite so bright. But his smile, though toothless, is as captivating as ever. And his high dome, shining with an ever deeper glow, reminds us that old age can bring wisdom. Gazing into that distant land where his peach ripens but once in six thousand years, he tells us that at a feast long ago we tasted its magic, and found something beyond Time and Space....

Unfortunately for others he speaks an unknown tongue. Some visitors in our home glance approvingly at other Chinese objects, but when they see the high-domed man, they stare.

"What a strange thing! *What* in the world is that?"

I laugh, unable to explain that he is not *what*—but *who*! That Shou Hsing Gung holds in his high forehead and gnarled hand all that our years in China gave us…

…so that today, when we read in the papers or see on the screen frenzied students anywhere in the world shouting, "Go home, Yankee!" they become to us, for a moment, Happy Harmony, and Ru-fu, Dai-hok and Ming-sing, as we first knew them in the heat of their revolt against the white man's world, and hear again their cry for recognition.

…so that today when we see the misery lined faces of refugees escaping disaster, anywhere, they are to us the refugees who huddled under the mat sheds in the chilling winter rains on the hill about our home by the White Pagoda.

…so that today, when we hear of young people training to "sharpen their tools to help their people…" or the people of some other land, they are Ding-chung with his magician hands, and Ru-fu, Dai-hok and Ming-sing, hoping to build a better and a free China—but against whom the odds were too great, the suffering to heavy, the understanding from the white world too thin.

When our guests, staring at Old Star Grandfather, say, "What a strange thing! Where did you find *that*?" I can only tell them, "He is Shou Hsing Gung. Yes. He is very strange! He comes from beyond the Western Mountains. And you have to travel a long, long way to find him."

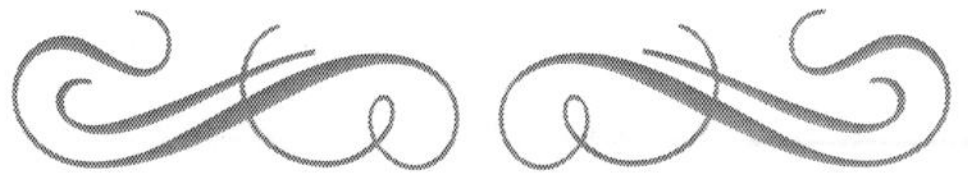

Acknowledgements

I thank my mother, who died in 1976, for leaving her unfinished draft of this book. She deftly described the situations and conversations in this text. Without her material this book would not exist.

I also thank Dr. Bill Brown of Xiamen University who distributed the manuscript to a number of his acquaintances involved with China. This led to contacts with several people intimately familiar with the locale and this period of China's evolution. One of Dr. Brown's books, *Amoy Magic*, plus other material he provided me, filled in background for Foochow. His website is www.amoymagic.com.

I greatly appreciated the insights that George D. Ngu, researcher of Foochow Mission History, provided to the conditions in China during this period, particularly the 1927 incident that forced my parents to flee to Formosa (Taiwan). He led me to John Caldwell's book *China Coast Family* and provided corrections to the Chinese expressions in this book. He confirmed that "no waves" and "no eggs" have exactly the same pronunciation. From George I learned that Mr. Ledger's dictionary of the Foochow dialect was published in 1929.

I would like to thank Jana L. Jackson, Beard family genealogist (Dr. Beard was president of Foochow College when my parents arrived), for providing excerpts of the Beard family letters that referred to my parents arrival and departure in Foochow. I learned from the letters that I was baptized by Dr. Beard in May, 1932! Dr. Beard's daughter, Kathleen, born in Foochow, returned to Foochow in 1988 and found that all the Mission buildings were gone. The White Pagoda and the Bridge of a Thousand Ages across the Min river were all that she recognized. The Beard family papers, prepared by Jana, can be found at yale.edu.

I greatly appreciate the efforts of James Bare, my editor at Tate Publishing. I could not have asked for better assistance.

Finally, I thank Ron and Ginny Kornafel for their careful scrutinizing of the manuscript and providing numerous corrections.